Go Your Own Way

First published by Dunce LLC in 2019

For general info: 4101 N Broadway #126
Chicago, IL 60613
Admin@duncecp.com
(775) DUNCE US
www.alexellison.com

Publisher's Cataloging-in-Publication Data

Names:	Ellison, Alexandra, author.
Title:	Go your own way : 7 student-centered paths to the best college experience / Alex Ellison.
Description:	Includes bibliographical references. | Chicago, IL : Dunce LLC, 2019.
Identifiers:	LCCN 2019902311 | ISBN 978-1-945028-25-0
Subjects:	LCSH College students. | College students--United States--Conduct of life. | Success. | BISAC EDUCATION / Student Life & Student Affairs
Classification:	LCC LB2343.3 .E45 2019 | DDC 378.1/98--dc23

Cover design by Laxalt & McIver
Book design by Adam Robinson for Good Book Developers

Printed in the United States of America

Go Your Own Way

7 STUDENT-CENTERED
PATHS TO THE BEST
COLLEGE EXPERIENCE

ALEX ELLISON

Dunce LLC
Chicago

For all parents.

Especially for my own parents,
who gave me the space to follow my dreams
and the love that reminded me I could.

Contents

T hough she sounded like many of my students as we began our first web call, the young woman on the other end of the line quickly took over the conversation. Amanda (not her real name) was one of those rare cases, a high school student who loved to talk as much as I do.

Often, my young clients are a little anxious—the experience of college selection and admission has become unnecessarily stressful, and usually the parent has reached out to me for help. Kids aren't usually enthused about baring their souls to a college-choice "expert," so I always plan on some getting-acquainted chit-chat before starting. But right out of the gate, Amanda turned the tables, asking me serious, probing questions about myself and *my* life. I found myself surprised and amused.

Amanda drove the hour-long call. The rapid-fire conversation was packed with talk about college tours, her GPA and test scores, her pressure-cooker high school, and her urgent wish to *not* make college *all* about academics. She spoke passionately about how she wanted to get away from home for college, and how she planned to *never* enroll in any college classes before 9 AM.

Finally, she paused for a breath. Sensing she was done sharing her thoughts, I asked her if she had any other questions for me.

"Yeah, I do," she replied, without hesitation. "You obviously went through all of this stuff yourself when you were my age, right? Well, why on *earth* would you want to do this all over again?"

I realized at that moment, to many students, the work I do has all the appeal of a prison sentence. It's the kind of job you might find on a reality show called *The World's Worst Jobs*, or even, *Jobs That Trigger PTSD*. College admissions, and for some, just the word *college*, can elicit feelings of despair, terror and confusion. Why *would* someone want to go through that experience more than once in a lifetime?

Perhaps it's my personality, which I've been told is ideal for an ER doctor—I find myself drawn to work that includes some urgency, and a dash of chaos. However, I think my career choice has more to do with frustration at the way things are, and hope for the way things could be.

In the US today, the experience of college selection and admission has all the earmarks of a mass panic. An entire nation of students (usually goaded by well-meaning but dangerously misinformed families) are stampeding toward the same handful of college gates. You know the ones—the notoriously selective, brand-name schools.

Somehow, we've brainwashed our college-bound kids (as well as plenty of others around the world) to believe that this is, if not the *only* way, the best way to get the education, the career, the *life* that they should have. The stakes, they're told, are incredibly high. Their future, their very *survival*, is at stake. So, not surprisingly, they're freaking out.

And rather than taking less-trodden paths toward not just hundreds, but *thousands* of other terrific schools, kids continue to fight and fret over the most stressful and tortuous paths. Worse, they have no idea if they'll even *like* what awaits behind the hallowed Ivy gate (or whatever other gate behind which they've been told success and glory await). That's not even part of the equation—they aren't stopping to think about whether or not they'll be happy there. All they are thinking is, *I. Have. To. Get. In.*

Ambitious, competitive students have realized that a vast number of their peers, all with the same level of merit as them, are sprinting toward the same handful of selective schools. So they become desperate to stand out, to be faster, better—even trickier—in order to gain admission. Students from privileged backgrounds are spending more money on test-preparation services, private consultants, and international service trips in order to have an even greater advantage than the ones they were born into.

Full disclosure: I am the owner of an education consulting and test-prep company. I mostly work with students from families with incomes above $100,000. You might expect that those families hire me because I flaunt a flawless record of getting students into Ivy League schools, but you'd be wrong. The truth is, I rarely work with students who have any chance of getting into an Ivy, or most importantly, would be happy and successful at one of those schools. I don't actually claim to be able to get anyone in anywhere. No, my real superpower is scouring for exciting opportunities that will fit the personality, talents, and passions of each student I see.

More often, my work consists of easing students and parents into a radical idea: *maybe instead of making yourself suitable for admission at a hyper-selective household-name university, you should be focusing on finding universities that are suitable for you.*

Private college-admission consulting is not affordable for the majority of families. However, I firmly believe that all students can benefit from participating in this process—so I've tried to make my services accessible to the largest number of kids that I can. Having a caring adult as a "guide on the side" can be both helpful and calming.

In addition to running my consulting company, I have worked with public schools in order to support counseling departments and serve more students. Unfortunately, as the number of counselors in public schools continues to decline, students are not receiving the guidance they need to explore all of the wonderful options available to them.

Depending on the state and the type of high school, student-to-counselor ratios of the US average around 500 to 1. As a result, many students make decisions based on the limited or anecdotal information they receive from family members and peers, which are often based on false or outdated information. Even the best-intentioned bearers of college advice too often begin their how-to prescriptions with, "What I think you should do," or "Here's what I did and it really worked for me."

Because of a lack of information about the wide array of higher-education options available to students today, students tend to continue to apply to the same 20 or so "brand-name" schools and those that are frequently referred to in the media. This means that the competition at these schools, which is already ridiculous, continues to get worse. In 2017, the University of California, Berkeley received over 85,000 applications, New York University received over 60,000, and Boston University received over 57,000. Several large universities hire outside "readers" just to sift through the volume.[1]

---

[1] https://www.usnews.com/education/best-colleges/the-short-list-college/articles/2017-09-14/10-colleges-with-the-most-applications

Worse yet, the college-admission process does not quite work the way we think it does. Colleges *love* to increase their applicant pools. Why? It means they can reject more students, enabling them to protect their "yield," the number of students who accept their acceptances. It turns out that this is a very important statistic to safeguard, since it factors into a school's selectivity. It's one of the factors used to rank schools in the ubiquitous, (and I would assert, infamous) *US News and World Report* college rankings. Yield is one data point, along with ratings for reputation, alumni giving, standardized tests, and faculty salaries.[2] In a recent satirical article in the *Chronicle of Higher Education*, Brian Rosenberg pokes fun at the rankings and the methodology used to compose them. He writes sarcastically, "Without The Rankings, one might have been misled by all the talk about the high cost of college into believing that colleges' spending less is desirable, rather than realizing that spending more, regardless of necessity, is a very good thing that results, through the wisdom of the special U.S. News formula, in a better position in The Rankings."

He continues, pointing out the great role money plays in the rankings by offering a sarcastic recommendation, "I suggest, therefore, that U.S. News determine the order of its lists not on the basis of some complex and mysterious formula, but simply on the basis of money: To the highest bidder would go the highest ranking." The rankings have heightened, not lessened (as might be suggested by the *US News and World Report*) the stress that surrounds college admission and "getting in." The hoopla of the ratings, along with the pats on the backs of colleagues at elite universities, is all quite silly and easy to see as a ridiculous American ritual.[3]

2   https://www.usnews.com/education/best-colleges/articles/how-us-news-calculated-the-rankings

3   https://www.chronicle.com/article/The-US-News-College/244325?cid=wcontentgrid

I started this work, independently, and outside of high school, in hopes of helping as many students as I could escape this mass panic. I wanted to help students and their families avoid spending too much money and winding up with ridiculous amounts of debt (a mistake I made myself). But the problem is a big one, and after five years of serving kids and families, I realized that I needed to amplify this crucial, potentially life-changing message: find the paths that will launch you and allow you to thrive, even if they are unheard of or underappreciated paths.

Who This Book is For

This book will be helpful for anyone interested in learning about more diverse paths to higher education, but my true mission is to bring this information to the people I call Guides: the parents, teachers, mentors, counselors, aunts and uncles, coaches, and older siblings of would-be college applicants. I firmly believe that if more of us were better informed about the real educational opportunities that await students today, we could all serve as college counselors to the young people in our lives. We could all help bring much-needed calm to the inexcusable chaos, stress, anxiety, and insecurity surrounding higher education.

In this book, I'll share the distinctive archetypes, or personality types, I've identified in my work with students, as well as actual case studies from my practice. Together, these will help illustrate the wide array of legitimate and rewarding paths after high school.

Keep in mind that I am not presenting these paths as the *only* paths, or these students as the *only* types of students who have found paths to college. Remember, people are a unique and ever-evolving blend of personalities, styles, preferences, and life experiences. My student archetypes are not intended to be student stereotypes, but guideposts and reference points for distinctive traits and sensibilities—patterns, if you will, that I've observed in my practice.

I invite you to use this book as permission to exit the higher-education rat race. It may feel like a risky choice, without a clear view of the road ahead. But I'll also debunk some of the myths about the life that one achieves by attending one of those legendary brand-name schools. Not surprisingly, the prevailing beliefs about the "cost-benefit" of a degree from these institutions can be wildly off base. In a world where we expect "disruption" in nearly every industry, when it comes to higher education most Americans are still blindly loyal to a handful of old-school (literally!) name brands.

My objective is to demonstrate that many exciting open gates await today's students…and I promise many of those gates will still take them through a few walls covered with that all-important, impressively verdant ivy.

CHAPTER 1

Why I Went to College

I was about 12 years old when I woke up early one summer morning to go garage-sale hunting with my mom, digging for the kind of cheap treasures that wealthy people discarded in Incline Village, the affluent community on the north shore of Lake Tahoe where I grew up. Garage sale-ing was definitely a verb in our family, describing the Saturday morning activity of scouring the newspapers for garage sale ads, paying close attention to those addresses we knew were homes of rich people, and driving up and down steep inclines in our aptly named town.

Incline Village is an exclusive enclave just over the Nevada border, where it attracts wealthy families who wish to leave California's state income tax behind (Nevada has none.) This lushly forested hamlet is where the well to do vacation and where the even more well to do reside, in woodsy mansions—log cabins on steroids—with access to private beaches and docks.

For most of my childhood, there was a town ban against nearly all fast-food joints and there wasn't a Starbucks until years later.

On this particular sunny Saturday, as I was getting out of the car, something shiny on the ground caught my eye. I reached down and picked up a broken and dirty piece of brown plastic with the word "HARVARD" etched on it in gold lettering.

Now is probably a good time to mention that back then (and to some extent, even to this day) I was imaginative, romantic, contemplative, and fantastical. I daydreamed, I believed in magic and fate, and I was deeply religious. I believed in Santa Claus longer than all of my friends and I loved the idea of an invisible guardian angel hovering over me at all hours of the day.

I desperately wanted to believe in fate and destiny and I wanted to feel…well, more important. Believing that some master guardian cared so much about little me as to map out my entire life and send me little hints and messages—communication that would direct me toward a future of total and complete happiness—certainly helped my ego.

So, when I tell you that finding a broken piece of plastic in the dirt was like a sign from God, *I am not kidding*. Laugh if you will, but it was a capital-S Sign that I dramatized, and one that served as a major catalyst in my adolescence.

I loved that little piece of plastic. I propped it up like a statue on a shrine. It sat atop my leopard-print painted desk, where I looked at it as I struggled with homework each night. I fervently believed that this little omen was there to keep me pressing on, as if I was some great warrior receiving divine inspiration.

I began to valorize my menial high-school struggles and I started to obsess over college planning (or more like college daydreaming, since I didn't really have a plan). When I was 15, my dad gave me a huge book of colleges for Christmas and I would flip through those pages, scanning for schools I'd heard of on TV or in the news, or schools that had old-fashioned, British-sounding names, or schools that were simply located in New England, because that place was supposed to be sophisticated. Anything west of the Mississippi, I thought, was not really a Serious School.

I confess, I exemplified the superficial college-bound snob. I wanted a distinguished college, a refined college, a college for smart people, and, let's be real: I wanted a college for rich people. That was a world I'd been exposed to in my hometown, and desperately hoped to enter.

The denizens of Incline Village fell into three main camps: people who worked in the service industry, people wealthy enough to not work (or who took periodic business trips to San Francisco) and retired (also wealthy) people. Some were full-time residents, others came for the summer and then again to ski in the winter. The San Francisco Bay Area's shiniest trophy wives headed to the Lake for the summer with their brood, while their CEO husbands flew in and out of nearby Truckee airport on the weekends aboard private jets.

My family belonged to the first of these groups. Though we were not wealthy ourselves, we were definitely part of the ecosystem of the wealthy: I babysat for wealthy families, my mom waited on wealthy patrons in restaurants, and my dad, who was a wine salesman, provided the fine vintages that wealthy people drank while they relaxed by the lake on vacation.

No one in my family ever resented those with money— quite the opposite. Though my parents never explicitly told us to strive for this lifestyle, it was clear that they really believed this lifestyle *could* be ours and *should* be ours. If there were financial struggles, my mom and dad hid them from us, and my youth was pretty much smooth sailing. What we needed we received, and we received most of what we wanted, too.

But here's the thing. While I'm grateful to have had parents who supported my dreams (and helped pay for me to reach them), I often wish they had questioned some of what I was pursuing, and challenged me to think more broadly about success. I convinced my parents that I was college bound and that the name of my future college mattered. They pretty much said, "Sure you can!" to whatever the goal of the day happened to be. They did everything they could to make up for what they didn't have or couldn't achieve when *they* were young. It was a classic but seemingly benign example of living vicariously through your kid.

While my grandfather was a University of Chicago graduate and a chemist, neither of my parents finished college. Each went for a year or so and then moved on to better things. My older sister didn't finish college either. No one told me where to go to college or how to get there. My parents didn't really talk about college—perhaps because they felt, based on my early and intense enthusiasm, that they didn't have to.

The day I found that broken piece of plastic was the moment I first had the idea that I *could* go to college—and that it *didn't* have to be the one over the hill in Reno, about forty-five minutes from where I grew up. Discovering that little sign in the dirt opened up my world and got me thinking more broadly about my opportunities, but at the same time, the gold letters that spelled out HARVARD narrowed my future path, and dramatically limited my view of success and achievement.

My parents had come to recognize the strangeness of our secluded, bubble-like community, and it concerned them. They decided it would be better for us to attend a high school with more "normal" kids from "normal" families. So when I was 14 and my younger sister was 8, they moved us to Minden, Nevada, a small ranching community on the other side of the Sierra Nevada mountains, about forty five minutes to the southeast of Incline Village. There were more kids my age there, not just retired couples or families who vacationed in Tahoe, and the pace was slower; life was simpler. But to me, that meant Mindenites were simple minded.

"These kids are backwards. They're just a bunch of hicks!" I declared to my mom. Alarmed by my snobbish stereotyping, she no doubt felt totally validated for moving.

I stubbornly refused to assimilate in Minden. I compared myself to other students and concluded that I was quite exceptional. While the local kids were out partying, I was usually studying, thinking all the while, "I deserve great things—look at me with my nose in the books!" I pushed onward, believing I was bound for the Ivy League and believing I was quite remarkable for my age.

Whew! Do you hate Younger Me yet? As I look back on that time, I find myself appalled and repulsed, too. But I also recognize now that it wasn't simply harmless adolescent self-involvement. It was a dangerous path. And that's why I do the work that I do, today.

I now understand where these beliefs about college and success originate and how they grow; I can see these same traits and beliefs in so many kids today, and while they often exasperate me, I have the perspective to empathize and understand. I get it. Unfortunately, parents are often guilty of fanning the flames, supporting and even intensifying these beliefs in their teens. Most of them don't realize it, though.

Parents play a critical role: they are the de facto go-to Guides and most accessible resources for teens who want to go to college. Despite a plethora of experts out there, kids still get the majority of their information about college and college majors from people they know and trust. And parents, naturally, may bring their own baggage: unrealistic expectations, or limiting beliefs and misinformation.

Before I graduated from high school, my restlessness got the better of me—I spent my senior year as an exchange student in Germany. It was from my small bedroom in a rural farming community smack-dab in the middle of the country that I applied to colleges back in the US. I took the two-hour train ride to Berlin to take my SAT and SAT Subject Tests.

How did my college story end? *Surprise.* I didn't go to Harvard. I remember logging into my Yahoo email account and getting the news that Harvard was a no-go. I got rejected from nearly all of the schools to which I applied.

Instead, I graduated from Northwestern University with a German Business degree and a heap of student loan debt. After the ceremonies and the pomp and circumstance, I drove back west in mid-June feeling utterly defeated. I did not experience the exuberant liberation I always thought I would after graduation. That destination that I'd always been aiming for and from which I'd expected such a great deal, was not as life-changing and success-bearing as I'd always believed. Surprise, surprise, the destination didn't deliver happiness.

Part of it *was* timing: I graduated during the Great Recession. Unemployment was rife, job prospects were dismal, and everyone was feeling pretty deflated. Believe it or not, I have never regretted my choice of major. The German part of my degree has been far more interesting and useful than the business part (and I own a business!) What I have regretted is what I paid (and am still paying) to get that degree. Was that necessary? But what I've come to realize is that the biggest misunderstanding on my part, was placing all of my happiness, self-worth, and hopes for success in a single place.

I went through a wild few years of deconstructing my old beliefs. It was a painful time of introspection, disappointment, and skepticism. I felt that I'd been lied to and fed false beliefs about college and...*life*. I came to realize that a degree was not a golden ticket "out" of any social class or situation. As I reframed my old beliefs, attempting to rebuild my life, I found myself growing increasingly bitter and cynical. I adopted an anti-college...anti-*everything* mentality.

As it turns out, I wasn't alone.

This was during 2010-2011, when groups like Uncollege and the Thiel Foundation were challenging higher education by offering alternatives. Uncollege was created by one of the first Thiel Fellows, Dale Stephens, who was a self-described *unschooler* as a kid. He tried college, but realized he could get more of what he wanted and needed to learn outside of the classroom.

Stephens left Hendrix College in Conway, Arkansas for San Francisco and after completing the Thiel Fellowship, which awards funds to students to start businesses if they forego college for two years, he started Uncollege. Entrepreneur Peter Thiel created the Thiel Fellowship to encourage students to forgo college in exchange for a 2-year incubator program and a $100,000 "for young people who want to build new things instead of sit in a classroom."[4]

Stephens wanted to encourage young people to learn, grow, and transform their lives outside of the classroom. Uncollege offered a high-touch residency program for students who knew they needed to get out of (or never go to) college but did not

---

4   http://thielfellowship.org/faq/

want to return to living with their parents. They offered students life-skills workshops, mentorship, internship placements, and travel abroad opportunities. Many other gap-year programs have emerged over the years, along with bridge programs and college alternative programs.

People began to come out and question the value of higher education, a trend that has continued to present day. There are blogs, books, and speakers who will blame higher education for the ill-preparedness of the youngest of today's workforce. Entrepreneur, blogger, and writer, James Altucher has written extensively about the subject with articles such as "I Failed to Prevent My Kids from Going to College,"[5] "Don't Send Your Kids to College,"[6] and "Living Life is Better than Dying in College."[7]

Students attracted to these alternative programs tend to be a very mature, self-directed bunch. But after awhile, I began to wonder if they believed they had to be in charge of their own education because no one truly understood them, that they were just too complex or different to even consider being among others in a learning environment.

I wondered if this kind of college-alternative thing was missing the point. Perhaps we didn't need an alternative to college, but a more affordable way to do it and more options for doing it. Furthermore, what most of these kids needed from the get-go was a caring adult who could provide advice and college suggestions based on their unique goals and preferences.

Higher education as an institution for learning is not the problem. College campuses are some of the only places left

5   https://www.slideshare.net/mobile/JamesAltucher/james-altucher-40-alternatives-to-college

6   https://jamesaltucher.com/2010/02/dont-send-your-kids-to-college/

7   https://jamesaltucher.com/2011/02/living-life-is-better-than-dying-in-college/

on earth where young people can incubate ideas, rub elbows with peers who will challenge, contradict and add to their own thinking, and ask big questions in a mostly safe space. I can't think of a better environment to brew up ideas that will advance us collectively as well as individually.

The problem is what we've done to higher education. We've charged too much for it, politicized it, and tried to make it more pragmatic, career-centric, and outcome-oriented. The American university has attempted to be everything for everybody and in doing so has made many very angry and resentful towards it. Creating a university that attempts to satisfy the liberal arts enthusiasts, the researchers, the careerists, and the athletes not only waters down the experience for students in each of these groups, it makes the college experience ridiculously expensive. Rather than honor college as a place of learning, growing, and questioning, we have scrutinized its return on investment, and measured it to the point of exhaustion, leaving us with what we have today.

I was 26 years old, doing research on the Swiss education system with a summer research grant from the Swiss Embassy. They had just come out with a new fellowship aimed at getting more Canadian and American students over to Switzerland to do research. I was working on my masters degree at the University of Nevada (yes, the very School Over the Hill that I'd been determined to avoid as a child!) and I wanted to learn more about how the Swiss education model got its nickname, *The Gold Standard.*

I brought my husband and toddler daughter along for the journey. So, while I did my research and conducted interviews, they hung out in our rented, third-story Airbnb flat in Mulhouse, France. The town was just over the border from Basel,

Switzerland, where my host institution was located—Basel was much too pricey for a two-month residency.

That particular summer was sweltering hot and air-conditioned buildings were hard to come by. Our little apartment had one stand-alone fan that we would move to follow us wherever we were sprawled out. One day, my husband, running out of cool places to go with a toddler, spent the day at Ikea with her.

But Basel is perfect. Actually, the whole country of Switzerland is perfect. Someone once told me they could never live there because the entire country is simply "too OCD." Indeed, an out-of-place blade of grass is hard to come by there. The place runs like a Swiss watch (sorry) and the people we met were remarkably happy (who wouldn't be with a minimum wage around $25 per hour?)

The Swiss are known for their outstanding *Dualausbildungssystem*, or dual education system, which consists of two primary tracks: the vocational track and the traditional university track. The vocational track is what the rest of the world has become so interested in. There is certainly a higher regard for vocational education in Switzerland, and students can earn advanced degrees in a number of different vocational pathways. In fact only about 30% of students there opt for the traditional university track, with the remainder choosing to pursue a vocation, which, by the way, can include business, banking and hospitality (which the Swiss are famous for), and baking and culinary arts, in addition to those career paths you might expect, like electrical and IT tracks.

I was very excited when I managed to set up an interview with Professor Dr. Antonio Loprieno, the past president of the University of Basel in northern Switzerland. Sitting in his office, Loprieno listened carefully to my questions and gave thoughtful answers. Then he said something that stunned me.

"In America, you see higher education as a form of emancipation. That is the difference between students in the US and Switzerland."

Wow. It was as if a beam of intense light had just revealed to me the real reason for my teenage ambition and my wildly romanticized pursuit of higher education. Loprieno was describing me, describing the hopes of liberation that I had pinned on reaching the magical place for which I'd set my life's course.

I didn't know this at the time, but for me, college meant emancipation—it was my ticket out. But emancipation from what? From what did I need to break free? I had a very comfortable upbringing. I grew up in the middle class, as a middle child, in medium-sized public schools. But I hated my place in the middle. I resented it. I wanted out of my nondescript life. I wanted to be propelled into something great, something dignified, something I had never come close to before. I *absolutely* saw an acceptance letter to an elite college as an acceptance letter into the upper class and into greatness. Getting into one of the "best" schools was my ticket out of mediocrity—probably my only means of getting out. To go where the majority of my peers would go, to go where "the majority could get in" would be, I thought, more of the same.

Why is the American view of higher education not as common in Switzerland and other countries, which have a more utilitarian concept of college's purpose? There are several cultural and political differences, but I believe that the most important is the powerful narrative, the collective belief, that *anything, absolutely everything* is possible for us. We've clung to the narrative that great riches are in store for us behind certain walls, and if we can only figure out a way to get to the other side of those walls, we'll be the lucky ones.

19

Fans of positive thinking, can-do spirit, and aspirational goal setting, hear me out.

I believe that the "anything-and-everything-is-possible" message is at once tremendously liberating and horribly debilitating. From the beginning of our country's history, ambition and upward mobility have been core values. Americans are taught to believe that our present-day positions are not set, but can get better—or worse. And in today's culture, the biggest key to our positions getting better or worse, to being a winner or a loser, is educational attainment. To improve, to *win*, requires educational attainment at a small group of very specific institutions.

So, as long as we are given examples of what *better* and *more* look like, we can strive for them. Students are plied with ivy-covered fantasies filled with exciting success stories of those storied schools' famous grads. This provides the hope and drive to push students forward—and toward the top.

I've come to recognize that this seemingly hopeful and aspirational belief system is a trap. The truth is, it puts most students in a terrible bind. They feel imprisoned, stymied; they worry they're in danger of being left behind. In this era of constant change, it seems almost improbable that a few big college brands still exert such a powerful pull on the imagination of high schoolers and their concerned parents.

There's a sumptuous banquet of higher-education options out there: over 3,000 4-year institutions and nearly 2,000 2-year institutions in the US alone. Yet many parents still seem convinced their kids will starve to death if they don't get into Stanford, Harvard, University of Chicago, Cal Berkeley, or the rest of the approximately 20 "best" schools.

There are a few exceptions which can loosen the staunch adherence to that list of the Best. If the school is one that neighbors and friends have heard of because of its reputation in sports or by a personal connection, or if it's one that may likely award a full-tuition scholarship to the student, it may be worthy of an application. It's not uncommon for parents to pull me aside and say something like, "Look, I'm OK spending $60,000 per year if it's at a school that we've all heard of, but if it's some generic state school, *they'd* better be footing the bill."

Much like how we now begin to think about what our Instagram photos from our vacation will look like before we've even embarked on the trip, we begin to think about how our friends will react to the name of the school our children will attend before they have even graduated high school. I think many parents can imagine nothing worse than eliciting blank stares or, "Huh. Never heard of that school," at the mention of their child's college name.

Does this sound a bit ludicrous? I've come to this conclusion by talking to hundreds of kids and their parents. Dissatisfied with the present, they fervently believe they can be set free from their current limitations by gaining admittance to an elite institution. And the more elite the institution, the more liberated, the more empowered, they believe they will be.

It's sobering to think how much magical thinking is going into the typical American student's choice of college—one of the most costly investments their family, and they personally, are ever going to make. That magical thinking has led to unhealthy approaches to college, obsessive behaviors among high-school juniors and seniors, and mania and hysteria (no, those words are not too strong—I've witnessed plenty of both!) around higher education in this country. Let's call it what it is: the Cult of College Prestige.

My mission is to help students and families understand that there are multiple ways to do this whole higher-education thing and to find success in life. A brand-name college degree does not automatically confer happiness, success, and safety.

That may sound like a self-help cliche, but here's the point: selecting a school must be first and foremost about the *student*, not about the college.

CHAPTER 2

We Are Not Dealing With Millennials Anymore

D o you cringe when I suggest that young people may actually need to be made to feel a bit more unique and special, when it comes to selecting the right school for them? ("What?! Those brats are entitled enough as it is!") Hear me out.

While that perception may have had some merit when it came to the Millennial generation (those born between roughly 1980 and 1994), this is not the age group we're working with anymore; these are not the students who are currently in high school and college. I can hear you asking, "Aren't all teenagers entitled, with inflated views of themselves and their abilities?" Maybe. Or maybe not.

Jean Twenge, PhD, a researcher and professor at San Diego State University, has done tremendous research on generational differences. In her book, *iGen: Why Today's Super Connected Kids are Growing Up Less Rebellious, More Tolerant, Less Happy—and Completely Unprepared for Adulthood—and What that Means for the Rest of Us,* she presents the newest research on this new generation, born between 1995 and 2012.

One of her findings is that teens today are much more practical, sensible, risk-averse, and realistic. These kids are going out less, which means they are drinking less, having sex later and learning to drive later, compared to previous generations. They seem to be doing less of everything outside of the home and more inside by themselves; so what on earth *are* they doing?

They are spending significantly more time in front of a screen than previous generations. iGen is the first group to consist entirely of tech "natives," people who cannot recall *not* having a computer or other digital device. Technology alone isn't the problem, but doing it in a sort of solitary confinement is. Even more troubling is avoiding the outside world, choosing instead the security and predictability of the game inside over the uncertainty of real life.

Twenge points out that this security-obsessed generation appears to be okay with lengthening adolescence, putting off traditional coming-of-age markers like drinking at a party or getting a driver's license. These realists view post-secondary education as a means to an end, with the "end" taking the shape of a good-paying job. They aren't as willing as their predecessors to engage in learning for learning's sake on college campuses, or to see value in majoring in those non-professional majors, like English, foreign languages, or history.

While parents of Millennials may have been pulling their hair out in 2005 when their sons and daughters insisted on majoring in Feminist Literature and joining the Peace Corps after graduation, parents today may be noticing their kids are remarkably sensible, well behaved, and realistic.

"Kids today are just *nicer,*" remarked a woman I sat next to at an event at the Swiss Embassy in Washington, D.C., where I was presenting my research about the Swiss Education System.

It was a subjective statement that may actually be backed up by some early research about iGen. However, what might appear to be "niceness," may actually be reticence and naïveté. Even though teens today are more compliant, more sensible, and less entitled, they are not necessarily more mature.

Meet the Homebody

"I'm not super excited about college. I mean, life's pretty good right now and I'm sort of afraid of leaving home. I know it'll be good for me, but...I don't know." While I thought Nora's sentiment was absolutely sweet and honest, it struck me that this is a *very* different sentiment than the one students voiced when I first started counseling.

Nora is not alone. More of the students I've worked with in the last three years have displayed more "homebody" behavior than the early iGen students I worked with just five years ago. Indeed, Twenge backs up my observations with some solid research on the subject.

This group of kids is growing up more slowly. They want to feel safe...all of the time. They try to avoid risk and awkward situations whenever possible. This is generally a good thing until it includes "sidestepping situations that might be uncomfortable, and avoiding people with ideas different from your own," as Twenge writes.

iGen's slower development and maturation has led them to want their college environments to be like home environments (but with more amenities, like climbing walls and lazy rivers). Twenge notes that they want "protection, safety, comfort, and home" and they want their school administrators to be more like parents. The trend to make universities more like deluxe residential resorts certainly did not begin with iGen, but it is clear that iGen is looking for more safety, security, and comfort in a college. This leads to a greater desire for safety and security in their futures.

Training or Educating?

The national argument we see today around the liberal arts versus vocational education—about how to best prepare young people for the future—is nothing new. Consider the debate around the turn of the century surrounding the best way to educate freed black men (educating women would come later) in a post-slavery America. Booker T. Washington was born a slave and he firmly believed that the only way for African Americans to reach equal status with whites was through technical, skills-based education. Freed slaves, he believed, would be made indispensable with more tangible skills.

Edward Burkhardt Dubois, on the other hand, was born in the north and had never lived in slavery. He was the first African American to receive a doctorate from Harvard and he believed, now that they had achieved freedom from shackles, African Americans needed to free their minds. DuBois believed blacks needed to pursue the same sort of *liberal* education that had always been reserved for elite white men.

The debate has continued with full force to this day. Individuals from both sides of the political aisle can be found on both sides of the debate—every time I think the issue is a political one, I hear a liberal and a conservative saying the same thing!

But by and large, it seems that iGen has sided with Washington; as a group, iGen is much more concerned about its future employment prospects than the Millennials. These kids are more likely to go after those more career-centric majors, such as finance, marketing, engineering, nursing, and management.

You can easily find examples of this by looking at enrollment numbers in various departments at colleges around the country. According to CNBC, the most popular major in the US is business, followed by majors in the healthcare field.[8]

Indeed, in my own work, I have noticed that business departments have become catch-alls for students with no idea of what they are interested in studying. Saying "I'm studying business," usually appeases the adults in the room and helps the student feel sufficiently satisfied with his maturity and discretion in choosing a college major.

The recent closures of college departments in the humanities are often in response to low enrollments in those subjects. Students today want to be able to see a very linear path from major to career (and a good-paying career at that). Unlike DuBois, they seem not to be as concerned with liberation of the mind; the idea of learning for learning's sake seems much more risky to today's teens.

This might also reveal something about the resurgence of Career and Technical Education (CTE) that we've seen in recent years. For example, Montana has doubled its funding for high-school career and technical programs and Nevada has tripled it. This is not a bad statistic on its own, and many of these programs also stress the "soft skills" that make students attractive to future employers, including communication skills, writing skills, and overall responsibility in the workplace, to name a few. It's true that students in CTE programs in the United States do still have to take core courses, like history, English, and science; and most who finish CTE programs do get jobs, for a while. That is, unless they become the victim of one of

8   https://www.cnbc.com/2017/12/15/the-6-most-popular-college-majors.html

the many middle-of-America company closures, outsourcing, or automation. Without the broader education needed to pivot and maneuver technological or economic shifts, these individuals may discover the hard way that career-focused training can be a self-limiting way to prepare for their future in the ever-changing Real World.

CTE has had an image problem in the US for many years. Schools have been accused of "tracking" students, i.e., putting minorities and students from low-income households on vocational tracks that require limited post-secondary education, and not adequately preparing students who may end up wanting to go to college. In many cases, I've observed these very things happening on the ground in schools—especially rural schools.

I have also seen many otherwise-uninterested students become more engaged in school once they were able to take some more technical, hands-on courses that had clear outcomes and objectives. We must remember that, as educators, our job is to provide options. We should not assume we know the best educational pathway for a young person.

It is no secret that many political conservatives, and others, have viewed higher education as an ivory tower, their faculties cabals of out-of-touch elitists. While this belief may be popular with many policy makers who want to direct more students toward in-demand careers, we are seeing an increase in the number of teens who doubt the value of a four-year college degree in non-career tracks. The message that non-career-tracked education is impractical resonates strongly with this very risk-averse generation. While questioning the value of a college degree demonstrates healthy skepticism, choosing not to pursue a four-year degree at all in favor of a short-term technical degree may be throwing out the proverbial baby with the bathwater.

So which came first—the policy shifts, or changing student demands? It's likely that teens are reacting to the income insecurity they saw during the recession; many teens saw their parents lose jobs, houses, and savings. They may have also seen older siblings graduate college with crippling debt.

However, there's another factor driving the popularity of more career-oriented majors: students who previously might have only needed on-the-job training or job-specific certifications are now obtaining four-year degrees for those same jobs. A good example is criminal justice, a degree that is fairly new to the scene, and one that's increasingly expected of students who want to pursue careers in law enforcement.

As Nate Silver wrote in the New York Times blog, *FiveThirtyEight,* "It would have been virtually unheard of 40 years ago for a student to receive a bachelor's degree in criminal justice or a related field. But these have now become fairly common majors, as more employers in these domains prefer—or even require—college diplomas."

While the iGen pragmatists may be commended for their careerist thinking and practical ambitions, they may also be missing out on something equally important: *learning.* Training and learning are not the same thing, and one is not more important than the other. I would also argue that *learning how to learn* should probably come first.

While training is linked to our vocations, learning transcends any one job and helps us throughout our lives as we move in and out of jobs and careers. It guides us in our hobbies, social interactions, political activism, service to our communities, and our leisure activities. Learning doesn't always have a clear outcome or a measurable output.

One need only look at the failures of our teach-to-the-test requirements to see how poorly our country understands the value of learning for learning's sake.

When you sit down to read a book (a book that is not required reading for school), do you outline the specific points you would like to be able to regurgitate after reading the book? So often, the things we learn while reading for pleasure, or simply going about our lives, are delightfully unexpected. I would not want our young iGeners to miss out on the discoveries that arise out of deep, sometimes seemingly pointless, learning.

Learning and training aren't mutually exclusive; in fact, the two practices must go together throughout our lives. Vocational training will not happen in a college philosophy class (unless you intend to become a professor of philosophy), but why would we expect that? Just because vocational training doesn't happen there, does that make that subject any less important?

Somehow, parents and students alike have come to expect the college experience to be *the* place where it all happens—our personal *and* professional development. While the liberal arts college in America generally does a great job at the personal development bit, it's not generally the place to look for professional development. Similarly, vocational training is highly specific and technical—personal development is not on the menu when you're learning how to code, for example.

The biggest difference between the two is that vocational training has to be updated and requires constant "upskilling" throughout our lives to match the rapid pace of technological change. In contrast, courses in the humanities, and much of the "core" curriculum of a liberal arts education, lay an enduring, "evergreen" foundation atop which lives—and indirectly, careers—can be built.

So one way to take pressure off our students is to let them know that *all* of their development will *not* happen in that four-year college environment. We must give them permission to learn about the subjects that truly bring them inspiration, enlightenment, and joy, and feed deep intellectual curiosity. There are ample opportunities for professional training and upskilling, including community colleges and the burgeoning array of online programs offered by companies like Udacity, Coursera, edX, and Udemy.

One of my favorite articles on this subject appeared in *The Atlantic* in April of 2014. Scott Samuelson, a philosophy professor at a community college, was gently teased by a random stranger whom he sat next to on an airplane. Upon learning what Samuelson did professionally, the man remarked, "So you teach Plato to plumbers?"

Because of Samuelson's unique situation, he is an ideal person to comment on the debate over the humanities in colleges today. Why *should* plumbers learn Plato? Or nurses, refugees, first-generation students, parents returning to school after having three kids, or anyone else, for that matter?

Samuelson's response was, I think, profound: "We should strive to be a society of free people, not simply one of well-compensated managers and employees. Henry David Thoreau is as relevant as ever when he writes, 'We seem to have forgotten that the expression "a liberal education" originally meant, among the Romans, one worthy of free men; while the learning of trades and professions by which to get your livelihood merely, was considered worthy of slaves only.'"

If all we're providing certain groups of young people is just enough training to get by in a job they may not like, making barely enough money to survive, we are enslaving them. Still, young people today may be more likely to opt for this path over the less conventional one because fear drives their decision making.

Counseling the Pragmatists

While counselors and parents of Millennials felt like they were constantly pulling them down from the clouds, today we are dealing with teens who don't have the same lofty future expectations. In fact, these students may be in need of "you-can-do-it" pep talks, and reminders that linear paths are rare. Teens should be aware that few people work in a field related to their majors, and that even becoming a nurse does not necessarily guarantee a lifetime of employment.

Naturally, these kind of conversations may elicit dramatic eye rolling or even freak-out responses from teens who are hunting for safety and predictability, and anxiously looking for a nice, solid, how-to answer. But offering them a "real world" view of what the college-to-career road looks like can also help them see the excitement and opportunity in ambiguity and uncertainty.

I'll be the first to admit that the future can look a little scary—even to an adult. The accelerated rate of job hopping, the dramatic increase in freelance workers, the relentless push toward automation of previously human-performed jobs, and the general uncertainty on the part of employers across all industries, add up to a situation that would astonish college-bound kids even one generation ago.

Part of preparing kids for the future workforce is emphasizing that an ability to "pivot," or change directions, and acquire transferable skills, are perhaps the best strategies to ensure their security and success in the future. It's actually quite ironic that today's teens are so pragmatic and linear, given the fact that there are so many new and exciting careers today that we didn't know about just 12 years ago. Jobs like drone operator, app developer, driverless car engineer, and big data analyst came on the scene within these teens' lifetimes, a perfect illustration of the importance of resilience and adaptability.

A 2016 article in *Fast Company* titled "The Four-Year Career" discussed the recent phenomenon of rapid job movement among Millennials, citing recent statistics that report the median time a US worker spends in a job to be just over 4 years. The average number of jobs a US worker will have a lifetime hovers around 11.

"Shorter job tenure is associated with a new era of insecurity, volatility, and risk," writes Anya Kamenetz.[9] Today, young workers think nothing of changing jobs every couple of years, often for better work and higher pay. Data also suggest that only about 27% of college grads are in jobs that directly relate to their majors.[10]

And before you say that this points to underemployment, consider all of the history majors working in investment banking, the English majors who are lawyers, and the biology majors who are working in sales.

When I present to a room full of parents and ask how many of them are in careers that directly correlate with their college majors, I may, at most, see two hands fly up in the air. There is plenty of reason to believe that major we agonized over choosing doesn't matter as much as we thought it did.

And if we're going to talk about preparing young people for the future, let's talk about why we're so focused on getting young people *employed* rather than *self-employed*. It's predicted that nearly 60% of our workforce will be made up of freelance workers by the year 2025. These are twisty, swirly, unpredictable times we live in, which means "thinking on your feet," and "turning on a dime," are behaviors that our teens must learn to embrace. Admittedly, it's a big ask for iGen.

---

9   https://www.fastcompany.com/1802731/four-year-career

10   https://www.washingtonpost.com/news/wonk/wp/2013/05/20/only-27-percent-of-college-grads-have-a-job-related-to-their-major/?noredirect=on&utm_term=.01a9a9d76650

The fact that we live in wonderfully uncertain times gives us even more reason to show young people the myriad ways to pursue post-secondary education. Knowing that you'll probably change careers frequently in your life could be terrifying to someone who expects certainty. But the flip side of that knowledge is absolutely liberating: understanding that this seemingly earth-shaking decision need not be treated as a do-or-die decision, but a step into the future—and probably the first of many steps, leaps, and pivots.

It's time to stop stuffing students into boxes that limit their futures. To assume that low-income, first-generation students are better off in vocational or technical programs or to assume that the daughter of a Yale grad is bound for Yale, is to lay the path toward disappointment and dissatisfaction.

It's also wrong to assume that a student who underperforms in math classes should avoid careers that require numerical-reasoning skills, that a C student cannot go to college and eventually earn a PhD, or that an AP student would never consider working as a skilled carpenter.

One of the best college entrance essays I ever read was by a student who intended to study political science in college. He'd taken mostly AP courses in school, but he wrote about the one class he took that allowed him to get into that "flow state" or his "element" and activate a different part of his brain. What class was it? Welding.

Now, who would think to ask this student to stop and consider the implications of this discovery? To take the time to explore what sort of paths might permit him to spend as much time as possible in that all-important flow state?

We must take the time to truly get to know our teens, rather than make assumptions about them, their abilities and, most importantly, what that means for their futures. As guides, we can help them discover their natural talents, define their passions, and as a result, help them chart their ideal paths for this next phase of their life. Those paths are the ones that will enable them to thrive, to be confident in their abilities, in college…and beyond.

CHAPTER 3

You Don't Know Yourself
As Well As You Think

" **I** suck at math."

This was Rebecca's mantra throughout high school. Leading a conversation with this statement shielded her from the anticipated ridicule or embarrassment; it was a sort of disclaimer, as if to say, "Let me just be upfront, my brain doesn't compute numbers—so now you know."

She believed in it so deeply that she planned on avoiding future work with numbers. It would be easy to accept her self-evaluations and move on with major, school, and eventually, career recommendations that suited Rebecca's self-assessment. However, what I love about the opportunity to spend significant time with each of my students is that we have the luxury of time to debunk myths—myths about a student's abilities, about the world of work, about college admission, and about math.

I like to start with an objective assessment of a student, then discuss the results without bias or judgement. Because I don't usually know a student before I start the process, I get to legitimately play dumb and let the student come forward in the most honest, authentic way.

"Really," I asked, "Is that what you think?"

I admit, I was messing with her and had to conceal the smirk coming to the surface. I had just downloaded her aptitude and interest assessment results and I knew something that she didn't about herself. She had created a label called *Sucks at Math* and basically stuck it to her forehead for the last several years, and I was about to peel it off.

YouScience is a research-based assessment that uses a series of brain games to determine real ability and authentic interests. Career recommendations at the conclusion of the test combine skills and interests, yielding results that students would hopefully be both good at and enjoy. I never want a student to "choose" a career based on this information, but these kind of results do give students some things to consider; they get to look at themselves in a new way and observe, as an outsider might, natural skills, aptitudes, and interests of which they may not have been aware.

In occupational guidance counseling, this type of process is called *Trait and Factor Theory*, and it aims to match people to their ideal jobs by analyzing individual differences and traits. Within this theory, several tests have been designed to match the characteristics of a student with the characteristics of a particular occupation. This kind of matchmaking can range from highly scientific trait-measurement psychology or differential psychology...to the utterly unscientific *College Matchmaker Game* used at local fairs and school events by Yours Truly.

The *College Matchmaker Game* consists of a giant banner with a series of questions like: Your favorite smell is: a) a campfire, b) soldering metal, c) a book, or d) anything new. There are then qualities that correspond to each letter. Players count the letters they selected and receive a card that corresponds with their type. Each card has a brief description of the type and a few College and Gap Year recommendations. It was fun to create, even more fun to use, and it got kids and adults alike considering colleges they'd never heard of, which is a "win" in my book.

It was decidedly *not* a research-based test. I thought the fun of it was pretty apparent, but at one event I had a dad ask me if it was based on any kind of real, scientific research. I explained to him that it was simply a fun way to share my research of hundreds of schools and the things I learned through my daily work with students. (He played the game anyhow.) The *College Matchmaker* is just as valid as one of those *BuzzFeed* quizzes, which my students often rely on more than actual science.

Back to Rebecca, our math-averse student. Her numerical reasoning test revealed that she was a "number predictor." While predictors aren't "number detectives," they are comfortable using numbers to solve complex problems, they are analytical, and they can spot numerical patterns.

While Rebecca may have "sucked" in her high-school math classes (she would point to a couple of C's on her transcript as proof), she actually possessed skill in numerical reasoning— arguably more important than numerical computation because calculators and computers have us beat there.

So, after a discussion about economics, statistics, data analysis, and related careers, Rebecca was interested and engaged. She realized that she was drawn to these subjects in a real-world context. She also recalled how she ran for and was voted in as Student Body Treasurer, and realized that she "always loved to work with money!"

This one aptitude assessment opened Rebecca's eyes to a world she had previously closed off to herself because of her own *self* assessment.

An objective assessment of a student's abilities, interests, work styles and study styles can lead to some powerful discussions, discoveries, and an even more optimistic outlook toward the future.

Rebecca later wrote her college application essay about this realization, observing, "Sprinkled throughout my life, there were actually signs that I am not only good with numbers, but I enjoy working with them," and she concluded, "This new-found knowledge has given me the confidence to search for careers with analytical components."

While Rebecca knew she wanted to study psychology, she wasn't yet sure how or if she would apply this interest in a career. I introduced her to the field of organizational behavior, which is related to Human Resources and addresses workplace behavior and relationship issues that may inhibit or help company growth. Rebecca loved the idea of combining enterprise and psychology. She began to see herself working in a business setting, but also helping people better understand themselves and each other. She began to picture herself crunching numbers to help a company grow, while ensuring the human-capital component was tended to as well.

Rebecca is now at California State University-Long Beach, and while she started off in human resources, she is now studying marketing. She told me over the phone she regularly refers back to her YouScience assessment. When she had to take Business Calculus in her first semester she admits, "It was *so* hard," but she added, "I can do hard math."

It was obvious this realization was a source of pride. This summer, she will travel to Thailand to take a management course and she hopes to get her Masters in Big Data and Social Media (yes, this is a real degree).

While Rebecca never doubted that she would go to college, she did doubt her abilities, specifically, her numerical abilities. By underscoring her abilities rather than deficiencies through an objective assessment (not a subjective mom-sessement, like the one given by the parent who says her son should be a lawyer because he likes to argue), her future path became a little clearer, and as a result, her confidence increased.

Many students doubt their skills, comparing themselves to their peers or people they see in the media. They tell themselves they are not *college material*. The problem is, they are often comparing themselves to a *particular* type of student who is on a *particular* type of path, in pursuit of a *particular* type of college.

The truth is, there really is no such thing as one type of "college material" anymore. There are more than enough four-year college options in the US alone, and American students are increasingly looking at international schools, opening up still more possibilities. According to recent statistics, the UK and Canada are the top two international destinations for US students, with 36% and 20% respectively. Compared to the US, the UK and Canada offer a bargain education, even with recent increases in tuition in these countries.[11]

There is, quite literally, a college for every type of student; and if a young person, perhaps with your guidance, cannot find an institution of formal learning (or just doesn't want to attend an institution of formal learning), there are many alternatives, which I'll discuss later, ranging from the military to gap year programs.

After President Obama's daughter, Malia, chose to do a gap year before college, the already-growing trend got some positive media attention, flipping on its head the old adage that

---

11   https://www.wsj.com/articles/why-more-u-s-students-are-going-abroad-for-college-1442800929

these kids will end up not going to college after their year off, choosing instead to live in their parents' basements. In an NPR radio discussion on Malia and the gap year movement, it was reported that in 2016, close to 40,000 students chose to do a gap year. There are many gap and bridge programs today that keep students engaged and active during their time away from school, with several that even award college credit. There's a San Francisco based gap year program called Year On which, lo and behold, is the rejiggered and rebranded Uncollege I mentioned earlier. They pivoted after realizing that instead of become an alternative to college, they could be more helpful serving as a *bridge* to college.

Gap year programs and other alternatives are not just for high-school students who barely graduated; in fact, many of the gap students I've worked with did quite well in high school. That is to say, these kids could reasonably be considered "college material" but they just chose not to go right away.

However, it is important to remind those students who have not succeeded in high school that college can be different than high school and that the majority of colleges in this country accept the majority of students who apply; C's, even D's and F's, by no means disqualify them from continuing their education. I'll highlight a few stories of students who were less than excited about going to college, yet found perfect fits and are thriving now.

The question shouldn't be if a student is "college material," but what material they are made of, and how that should inform their unique path after high school. When we give students generic "guidance" that leaves them feeling like they are part of a herd they don't belong to, they become discouraged and confused about the process of applying for college.

For example, if a counselor presents a student's best option as the local state school and she can't picture herself there, she may stop seeking advice altogether. If her parents keep talking about Georgetown, because the neighbor kid went there, and that doesn't feel like a fit either, the student may just stop looking to her parents for guidance and support too.

Unfortunately, the student may be left to figure things out on her own, possibly missing some wonderful hidden gems that she may have discovered if guided by a caring adult who helped her envision her own, unique path.

Every student needs to be shown that there are specific colleges, programs, and opportunities that are absolutely ideal for their unique personality, strengths, and interests.

When my first box arrived from the new clothing company Stitch Fix, I instantly understood the appeal. The recipient feels special, taken care of, and unique when she opens her box of custom-selected clothes, shoes, and accessories.

There are now many companies like Stitch Fix that "hand select" pieces ideally suited for you (often things you would have never considered before), based on an inventory you complete online. Not only does this inventory collect body measurements, it also collects information about your lifestyle, job, activities, and preferences. The idea that there are "experts" who can curate the ideal outfits for our lifestyles and body types feels quite special. Even if there is no real "science" to this work, it feels intimate and personal. More importantly, that feeling of being *matched*, makes us feel that we all have wonderful "fits" out there, just waiting to be discovered.

This process of personalized matchmaking is exactly what's been lacking (and what I've devoted myself to providing) in the college-admissions process. Young people need options that are uniquely suited to them, rather than be told that if they don't fit into a size 2, look good in yellow, or feel itchy in wool, they are out of luck.

We assume that every student strives for Harvard and that most land somewhere "below" that ideal. Imagine if your whole life revolved around trying to get into a size 0! (Oh wait, I just learned there are people who do that…)

Imagine how different this whole endeavor would feel (not to mention what would happen to the crazy-high anxiety levels) if we took the time to discover each student's unique personality traits, interests, and skills, and presented appropriate post-secondary options based on those traits. How special would students feel upon learning that their path does not look like any of their peers'? How comforting would it be to let go of the agonizing comparisons?

That vision is what compelled me to start my company, and to write this book.

CHAPTER 4

Meet the Student Archetypes

W e love assigning "types" to ourselves. We love the clarity and simplicity of labels and typologies. We gravitate to those simple, click-bait tests on *BuzzFeed* like, "What Disney Princess Are You?" or "Which US City Should You Live In?" Even though we rationally know a 2-minute quiz should not dictate major life decisions or that Disney Princesses are not actually *real*, we think maybe, just maybe, a little insight or epiphany might come from that quiz we take on our lunch break or before bed.

Some people discount even the research-based aptitude and interest assessments like Myers-Briggs, Emergenetics, or YouScience (my assessment of choice), writing them off as meaningless or limiting. They blame them for "pigeonholing" people and limiting their choices.

I've shared humorous stories with friends who, after taking the ASVAB (Armed Services Vocational Aptitude Battery test) in high school, or some similar test, were recommended careers for which they had zero aptitude or interest. An agnostic German teacher I know was given the career recommendation of rabbi as a kid, and a medical researcher friend was told she should be an artist. (I should mention that both are happy in their current professions.)

A former colleague told me she had never taken aptitude tests seriously because she has always been able to "game" them, getting different results each time because she could predict which questions would lead to the results she *wanted* to see. (I wondered why one would want to "game" these tests if the result is to better understand oneself!)

Another colleague told me she was sort of afraid of taking these kinds of tests because she was worried the results would *tell her* that she was in the wrong profession.

What I know is that in my work with teens, an objective test—one that does not ultimately care if you become a dentist like mom, or a lawyer like Uncle Ray, or go to USC because you're a "legacy" there—can be a great starting point for a young person trying to peer beyond the familiar circle in which he has grown up and gone to school.

The right test (guided by a caring and competent adult), can offer some ideas, nudge a student forward, and inspire action. A guide can also help make connections where there appear to be none. It's important to let teens know that the path can and will change, and that it's okay! The important thing is that they feel that they have some direction right now— even if that direction changes 180 degrees tomorrow. There is an incredible sense of confidence and joy that emerges when we know we have a direction to walk in at this particular moment in time. Walking forward is better than not going anywhere, or feeling stuck. Walking forward opens up new vistas and new choices, as well.

Getting "unstuck" is the first step. The next step is to give yourself permission to change directions, and not just once, but as many times as is necessary in this exciting and unpredictable life. The real value in these tests comes from their ability to shine a light on qualities (perhaps some never before acknowledged) that make a person feel confidence, pride, or excitement, and inspires those who feel stuck to take the first step in a new direction.

I tell students not to get too hung up on the specific career recommendations that result from their assessment, but to focus on the types of career *activities* that are recommended, as well as the skill and interest results. Perhaps someone could have helped my teacher friend see some qualities of a rabbi in teaching, or my research friend a bit of art in medical research. To feel good about our abilities is the first step; after that, we have the motivation to get going.

So maybe those *BuzzFeed* tests aren't so silly after all, if they get you thinking about ways to improve your life, your work, and your relationships.

Why Archetypes?

The idea of archetypes was pioneered by Carl Jung, who believed that all of us have dominant types, which we express through patterns in our decisions, values, and traits. Carl Jung's original archetypes were Hero, Creator, Explorer, Outlaw, Jester, Lover, Caregiver, Everyman, Innocent, Rule, Sage, and Magician. Since then, others have used these and other archetypes in a variety of settings for a variety of purposes, including psychotherapy, career counseling, business coaching, and branding.

Cerries Mooney, a branding expert who helps "solopreneurs" identify their archetypes in order to create more meaningful brands, describes archetypes this way: "What an archetype 'is' is hugely subjective. To me, an archetype is a perspective. It's an angle of looking at myself that has been cultivated throughout the generations before me."

The widely used Myers-Briggs Typology Indicator or MBTI is a personality test that results in one of 16 personality types. This test uses a four-letter naming model (I'm an ENFJ), with each letter representing a specific personality aspect. The combination of traits leads to one of 16 typologies. The site 16personalities.com offers a framework similar to MBTI and provides a free personality test on their website.

According to the company, "Personality is just one of many factors that guide our behavior...our actions are also influenced by our environment, our experiences, and our individual goals. We outline indicators and tendencies, however, not definitive guidelines or answers."

I have created a "pantheon" of Student Archetypes from observations I've made during my five years of working with kids. They include:

- The Achiever
- The Artist
- The Adventurer
- The Specialist
- The Hero
- The Skeptic
- The Independent Learner

Some of the archetypes I've created for this book mirror the original archetypes outlined by Jung, such as Hero, Creator, and Explorer. They are intentionally simplistic titles, but the people behind them are definitely not.

I created these seven student archetypes based on work with many different kinds of young people. These are the types I've seen the most and for which I have some compelling and demonstrative case studies. Their stories offer wonderful insights and resources for other students. Most students, in fact, will be a hybrid of multiple types—that's normal. Glean what resonates from each of the archetypal stories in order to find the right blend for you or your student. Once again, the seven archetypes are not meant to pigeonhole students. Instead, they offer a path on which an individual could envision themselves walking, and eventually sprinting.

These archetypes are by no means *all of the types.* They suggest unique ways to "Do College." While college may seem like a destination, (even the phrase "go to college" reinforces this mindset), the pursuit of education is an *action.* But it's easy to see why people have gotten confused, especially when most educations take place in a...*place.* Rather than encouraging my clients to pictures themselves *somewhere,* I encourage them to envision themselves engaged, in action.

I recommend taking the Student Archetype Quiz on my website[12] and receiving your Custom College Plan for your type. You'll probably see yourself or your student in more than one of the archetypes. Most people identify with a blend.

While it's great to see yourself or your student in an archetype—I think you'll relate to at least one of these students' stories—keep in mind that none of these should be viewed as a strict blueprint. Everyone's story is different, but everyone's story also offers nuggets of wisdom or bits of information that resonate for us and inspire us. I hope these stories offer the assurance that each path, each college choice, and ultimately, each life is the right one...for you.[13]

---

12   https://alexellison.com/quiz

13   Resource: http://www.soulcraft.co/essays/the_12_common_arche-types.html

"I THOUGHT I WOULD BE MORE OF A LEADER IN HIGH school...then I realized a lot of the "leadership" kids weren't very serious about school." Caroline and I talked on the phone the summer after she graduated from a private religious school. From her rural home along the Sierra Nevada mountain range, we had to switch to Facetime audio for a better connection.

Caroline's familiar, sing-song voice chimed on the other end; her high-pitched, cheerful greetings and her reflexive "thank you" following any comment that could be a possible compliment, told me why Caroline was so well liked by her peers and teachers. She was nice to everyone...except, at times, to herself.

Full disclosure here. I am an Achiever, so this chapter hits close to home for me. I was the kind of Achiever who equated her entire self-worth to the name of the institution to which she was accepted. My whole identity was wrapped up in that of my future college.

I would be the first one in my family to get a college degree, so even when I just talked about college, my parents made me believe I was pretty special. And such a special kid certainly deserved a special college. Special colleges were the ones found in the *US News and World Report* Top 20 List—those schools that admit a tiny percentage of applicants.

So simple was my thinking around college that I didn't even really discuss college cost with my parents. We were going to "figure it all out" along the way.

Because I can so intimately identify with the Achiever, I feel equal parts frustration and empathy for these types of students. I hear them say things like, "But is that really a *good* school?" or "If I don't get into a really *good* school, I'll feel like all of my hard work in high school was for nothing," or "I don't get it! Suzie got into that school and she didn't even do that well on the ACT, but I got a 32 and didn't get in!"

When I hear these remarks, I so badly want to "go deep." I want to talk about not comparing themselves to others, because this leads to the trap of insatiable striving. I want to tell them that they can create their own measuring sticks, and not wrap their self-worth around an admissions decision over which they have little control. I want to tell them to watch Steve Jobs' commencement speech, especially the part where he says "you can't connect the dots looking forward; you can only connect them looking backward. So you have to trust that the dots will somehow connect in your future."

Then, instead, I put my "Sage on the Stage" persona in check. I know that if someone had told me these things when I was in high school, I would have ignored the advice, convinced that my determination and hard work would be and *had to be* rewarded by admission to an elite university.

To be fair, the kind of determination found in Achievers can have wonderful benefits in life—hard work and determination are generally commendable attributes. But paddling too hard, too soon, also has its risks. My deep disillusionment after completing college was a perfect example. My intense efforts had not been rewarded in the ways that I expected. The "gap" between my expectations and my outcome turned out to be a very deep chasm, which I spent another five years figuring out how to cross.

As part of that painful process I had to learn, on my own, how to put my Achiever attributes in check. Not every Achiever will, even with expert guidance, be able to cultivate the self-awareness needed to avoid such pitfalls. You're not just dealing with a personality style, but an entire culture. If you're a Guide, remember that you alone can't expect to stem the tide of misinformation and peer pressure that these young people are subject to.

The young Achievers we are working with may have to walk a similar path to mine, moving from magical thinking to reality at their own pace and on their own terms, following some difficult life lessons. So let's look at what we can do to support Achievers and how we can harness those powerful personalities to help them "do college" in a way that feels fulfilling and authentic.

It was predetermined that Caroline would go to the one private, Catholic high school in her area. Her family thought this was simply the best school around. She would wake up early to make the 45-minute commute to school, and she would endure the pressures that came with attending a school where virtually every other student was aiming toward the same very high, very small, target.

In this climate, students become masters of comparison, judging their own intelligence, athletic abilities, extracurricular involvement, and likeability in relation to their peers.

"I always dreamed of Harvard and Stanford," said Caroline. "I always wanted to do the best I could."

After freshman year, Caroline recalls the stress becoming more real. Her parents would joke with her that if the stress became too overwhelming, she could always just go to the local public school. That didn't happen.

The summer before her freshman year, Caroline decided to adopt a healthier diet and exercise habits. She told me that summer boredom prompted her to take on a new project: her body. What started as a healthy habit quickly became an obsession and her low calorie intake reached a dangerous tipping point, resulting in mental and physical fatigue. But she pressed on, wanting to do the whole diet and exercise thing like a straight-A student would: perfectly.

As sophomore year began and homework was piled on, Caroline admits, "It was a big jump for me." She began obsessing over academics. She would work harder than she really needed to, reviewing her honors chemistry notes for hours. Caroline directed her obsessive habits toward studying. At the same time, the dieting that began in the summer became more dangerous. Caroline had always enjoyed cooking, but she began cooking for friends and family with newfound fervor, finding comfort in being around food but not allowing herself to eat it.

Before Christmas break of her sophomore year, Caroline was diagnosed with an eating disorder. She struggled through sophomore year, seeing a nutritionist but still maintaining her obsessive attitude toward food *and* school. In the summer after her sophomore year, Caroline's mom and nutritionist thought it would be best if Caroline was admitted to a recovery facility.

"The deal was that on our summer vacation, if I did well and maintained my weight, I wouldn't have to go to the facility." Caroline, still upset to this day, shared with me that she felt she *did* do well and she was really quite proud of herself. "But even though I did do well, my mom and nutritionist still decided to admit me. I felt so blindsided."

Caroline believes this was likely the plan all along, and she still feels a sense of betrayal. While she sees several negatives in her treatment center, like the rule about no exercise, she admits that there were positives that came with the experience. She made new friends, she discovered mindfulness, and learned about Obsessive Compulsive Disorder (OCD).

According to the International OCD Foundation, "Numerous studies have now shown that those with eating disorders have statistically higher rates of OCD (11% – 69%)...In 2004, Kaye, et al., reported that 64% of individuals with eating disorders also possess at least one anxiety disorder, and 41% of these individuals have OCD in particular."[14]

Caroline began to think about her past; even before the eating disorder, she had obsessively washed her hands, prayed, and told the truth. She began to recognize that these habits formed not just because she was a good and obedient kid; she began to realize that OCD had been there her whole life. When she was in school, her OCD "grabbed onto" her academics, and when she was out of school, it latched on to diet and exercise.

I asked Caroline if she thought going to a less competitive school would have made a difference. She told me that while her particular high school environment fanned the flames, she believes her OCD would have caused her to obsess about any number of other things, even if she did attend that local public school.

In fact, Caroline has very few regrets today. She believes that this experience actually taught her a lot about herself and life. Indeed, Caroline talks with the kind of maturity often reserved for someone late in life.

"Find worth in things other than grades and test scores, and find *other ways to determine your self-worth* besides grades and test scores," she advises kids today. Her advice to parents? "Don't be condescending toward kids' emotions and experiences. Validate their feelings."

---

14 https://iocdf.org/expert-opinions/expert-opinion-eating-disorders-and-ocd/

She has also become a big proponent of mindfulness and meditation, practices she believes students should start learning in elementary school. Learning how to sit still and do nothing is really hard for some kids. Caroline admits that to this day, when she has nothing to do, she can start to feel depressed. She works on this daily.

Finally, she has learned to be more vulnerable and to break down the false, pretty, and unrealistic images she previously portrayed. In doing this, she believes, we build stronger relationships with others. In a brave act of vulnerability, Caroline has started a new blog, *La Beuté d'Être*[15], where the French translation for "the beauty of being" reminds us to revel in the glorious action of being alive.

While I'm moved by Caroline's new-found inspiration and wisdom in the aftermath of a painful experience, I hope that students can access these revelations without coming as dangerously close to death as she did.

For Kimberly, going on a service trip during spring break of her junior year put things into perspective; she began to realize that she didn't want to be part of the rat race and all of the typical hoopla around college admissions.

Throughout the school year, Kimberly could regularly be found crying in her bedroom. The source of her tears? Sometimes it was her AP homework and the AP practice tests, on which she always seemed to fall short of the 4 she so desperately wanted. Sometimes it was her ACT scores, which hovered just under a 30, as if taunting her—she so badly wanted that 30!

Whatever the cause of her pain on any given day, the underlying reason was comparison. She compared her grades, practice test scores, ACT scores, summer plans, and everything

---

15   https://labeautedetre.wordpress.com/

else to those of her peers. Even if she felt good about a grade, a score, or a plan, she was sure to feel badly as soon as she talked to her friends about what they were doing.

Though it was not the case with Kimberly's parents, some parents of Achievers exacerbate the challenges their kids face by actively participating in the comparison competition. Social media makes comparing our children to others' children that much easier. I've seen parents erroneously claim their children were National Merit Finalists on Facebook, or post pictures of their children in front of Ivy League schools on their college visits, with captions like, "Wouldn't it be so amazing if she got in!?"

It turns out parents talk...a lot...to other parents. Parents frequently email and call me, concerned that a friend's son did xyz but still didn't get into Dartmouth, or that another friend's daughter had a perfect ACT score and didn't get into any of the schools on her list.

"What does this mean for *my* kid?" they wonder.

I recently spoke with a dad who was worried about the pressure his daughter was feeling to perform well on her ACT retake. "This kind of thing sends her over the edge," he said of his Achiever daughter.

Yet he was equally concerned that there were not enough "brand-name schools" on his daughter's growing list of colleges.

"I haven't heard of any of these colleges!" he protested.

As parents, we can do a lot to calm the negative side effects of the Achiever personality while also harnessing the positive aspects of that archetype. Parents of Achievers have to be very aware of their kids' tendency to compare themselves to others, and not add to the mania. While parents of other types of students may want to point out the work ethic of a friend's kid as a way to motivate their own kids, parents of Achievers should avoid comparisons completely.

Achievers rarely need to be pushed, but they may need to be picked up after a fall; Achievers can fall hard. While you may think nothing of your daughter's B, she may see it as the final straw that will completely ruin her life.

I applaud parents of Achievers who build in "distractions" for their Achievers, such as family vacations, volunteer projects that can be done as a family, or sports. I think anything that shows the Achiever that there is more to life than academic achievement and college acceptances is a good thing.

In the refreshingly light-hearted book, *How to Be A High School Superstar*, Cal Newport follows the high school paths of a few students who chose to not participate in the madness that many young people experience in pressure-cooker school environments. While so many students believe signing up for more, taking on harder classes, and putting in more hours will inevitably lead to greater success, Newport showcases students who did the opposite and still got into the colleges they wanted, finding balance and happiness in the process.

Too many students do *more* in order to appear more interesting on their college applications; however, as Newport hypothesizes, "Interestingness cannot be forced or planned in advance. It is generated, instead, as a natural by-product of "deep interest," which is a long-term pursuit that a student returns to *voluntarily and eagerly* whenever given a chance."

While many students and parents are looking for how-to guides in order to stand out in the college admission process, the truth is, if "interestingness" has to be forced, then it isn't that interesting after all (and it will end up exhausting you). Newport demonstrates through case studies that students who have sufficient downtime and free time outside of school are more likely to develop interests, which, lo, often lead to "interestingness."

It's also a good idea to introduce Achiever students to different adults who have followed their own paths to success, in order to show them that there is more than one one way to thrive in life. Introduce them to people who have led happy and fulfilling lives even though they didn't go to an Ivy League school (or maybe *because* they didn't go to an Ivy League school).

In his groundbreaking book, *Where You Go Is Not Who You'll Be*, Frank Bruni, a journalist and long-time writer for the *New York Times*, demonstrates that throughout history, some of the most "famous" and recognizably "successful" figures have gone to "off-brand" or less-selective schools. Unfortunately, Bruni's book sometimes reinforces certain stereotypes of success; he notes that the well-off people in his book often end up at Harvard, even if they started at an unknown state school (again, perpetuating the idea that Harvard is the Gold Standard).

However, I still think this is a good book to read with students, and to use as a jumping-off point for discussing the various paths people take. Even the people you've heard of often went to schools you may haven't heard of. The book is full of examples that demonstrate there is life beyond the Ivies; that going to a school other than that vaunted Top 20 does not relegate you to living in your parents' basement.

While we know the world isn't this black and white, for Achiever teens, things can often be all-or-nothing. They are just exiting childhood, when parents often provide instruction in exactly those terms: right and wrong, good and bad. High school students lack a large enough set of life experiences, which ultimately teach us that there are endless shades of grey in between the extremes. As well, Achievers are not generally comfortable with nuance, because of the uncertainties and ambiguities that come along with it. Achievers think in terms of winning and losing. (Want to exasperate an Achiever? Use the word "maybe.")

It can be helpful to show Achievers the sometimes circuitous routes many successful people have taken—especially people they admire. I once worked with a transfer student who was convinced he had to go to one of the country's most selective colleges in order to get into the world of finance and investment banking. Even after he shadowed an investment banker who had become CFO of his company and who had attended his local state school, this student was *still* not totally convinced he could opt for anything other than a school on the list of *US News and World Report* Top 20 schools.

So, this could take a bit more work and a few more introductions. And even though it might make you cringe to use the example of Mark Zuckerberg dropping out of Harvard to find his "success," keep in mind that you need to meet your student where she/he is *currently*; your student's view of success might be different than yours, and your student's heroes might be very different than yours.

Many kids in the iGen cohort today are followers and admirers of social activists, social media celebrities who advocate for justice, and companies that do good for people or the environment. You might mention someone like Franchesca Ramsey, who is a social justice advocate, comedian, writer, and YouTuber who first attended an art high school, then tried studying acting, then switched to graphic design. The British rapper, songwriter, and activist, M.I.A, or Mathangi "Maya" Arulpragasam, grew up during the Sri Lankan Civil War and lived in extreme poverty as a child. She attended Central Saint Martins College of Art and Design in London and became a renowned stencil graffiti artist.[16]

---

16   https://web.archive.org/web/20080513082654/http://niralimagazine.com/2004/10/not-so-missing-in-action/

Stories like these can be both inspiring, but can also offer a dose of realism and perspective that will likely resonate with Achievers.

For students like Caroline, at the extreme end of the Achiever spectrum, finding schools with the right support services is paramount. Make a point to inquire about these services on college visits and even schedule meetings with student counseling centers. Make sure you ask about fees for such services, as some schools will charge extra and others make them available at no additional cost.

Some students will want to maintain contact with their home therapists, nutritionists, and other practitioners, so ask them about virtual meetings or phone calls while your student is away at school. Some students may require ongoing care with local providers, so have early conversations with your student about the importance of applying to local schools.

While most schools out there today will offer some kind of support, or at least be able to refer students to resources in the community, students have to be self advocates in college, which may not have been necessary in high school. This goes for students who have Individualized Education Plans (IEPs) in high school and who might be accustomed to a certain amount of hand holding or parents and teachers "keeping an eye out" for them.

In college, students will need to become comfortable asking for and maybe even demanding the support they need to be successful. This level of agency is taught and learned, so it's wise to start practicing now.

Guiding the Achiever

Caroline knew she had to tell her story…the whole story. This major challenge was impossible to ignore in over a dozen essays that all have prompts like, "Tell us about a challenge you've overcome," or "What life challenges have made you who you are today?" or "What did you once believe to be true that you no longer believe?"

Not only was it unavoidable, it was necessary to let the college admission officers know why Caroline did not do a fancy internship, service project, or volunteer work throughout much of high school; she was obviously preoccupied with more pressing concerns.

When parents ask me if their kids should write about things like eating disorders or mental health challenges, my first question is, "Does the student feel comfortable telling that story?" My second question is, "Does the student *want* to tell *this* story?"

While Caroline clearly sees her diagnosis, treatment, and ongoing struggle as formidable and character-building experiences, not every student will see the same experiences the same way.

Students will also judge different experiences in their lives as being formidable, so I don't believe we should tell them which are and which are not. When parents express concern that their child might not gain admission to a particular school if an experience is disclosed in an essay, my response is, "If a school rejects your child because they learned about a significant and formidable experience in his/her life, then thank goodness you found out now that this was not the right school for your kid."

It can be hard for all young people, especially the Achiever types, to be vulnerable in their college essays. While writing about themselves shouldn't move students to the point of large-scale discomfort, it is likely to feel unnatural, especially if they've never had to do it in school. Admitting past failings or wrongdoings, sharing insecurities, or taking blame for a time they've wronged someone are tough feats and they are exactly what makes applicants more human and relatable, just like they make all of us more human and relatable. We can help Achievers see the strength that comes from vulnerability, and the college essay is a great way to teach this skill.

While not a good option for everyone, sometimes Achievers need to literally remove themselves from the comparison trap by not participating in the US College Admissions game. By playing in a different arena, and not applying to the same schools that all their friends are, many students cultivate a healthier outlook.

Many schools in the UK and in Canada (where more and more US students are looking) have very black-and-white admission standards. For example, they'll let students know, "Don't bother applying if you don't have these test scores and this GPA." While this may sound harsh, it's actually a breath of fresh air, compared to the very hazy and ever-changing US admission standards.

American students and their families know that US college-admissions practices are infuriatingly subjective. No one really knows what it means when they hear that admission representatives look at the "whole student." The opaque and inconsistent process of admissions can give false hope to students with poor academic records and an unfair advantage to students who can tell a good story.

I've worked with Achiever students who've told me they appreciate how direct and objective some international admissions practices can be. It's nothing personal when a college's website states, "US applicants must have 3 AP exams with scores 5 and a GPA of 3.5."

Students know that they need not apply if they don't meet those criteria, which can actually provide a level of certainty and clarity that students, especially Achievers, find comforting.

Finally, Achievers, more than any other type, need a life outside of school. Help encourage this by speaking their language; tell them that the most competitive colleges have enough 4.0 students and they need more interesting students. You don't become more interesting by collecting more As; you become more interesting by collecting more experiences.

Tips and Tactics for Supporting the Achiever

- Try your best not to compare your student to others; they are likely already doing that on their own.

- Help your Achiever step outside of the US colleg-admission mania by introducing him to international schools.

- Talk to your student about taking some time off before college and doing a well-organized gap year program. Share with them that these programs attract lots of Achievers, like themselves, and that doing a gap year is a positive alternative. Check out gapyearassociation.org for a full list of vetted gap programs.

- Help Achievers redirect their ambitions to activities outside of school; let them experience achievement in non-academic pursuits.

- Encourage your student to participate in activities where "the chance for achievement is very low, but the chance for personal growth is very high," - Patrick Hayashi, former associate vice chancellor for admissions and enrollment at the University of California at Berkeley, in the documentary *The Test and the Art of Thinking* (a great film for Achievers and their parents).

Sample College List for the Achiever

The key should be recommending schools that will resonate with the Achiever mindset and personality while also recognizing that Achievers may benefit from a supportive, yet challenging environment that allows them to be themselves and thrive at their own pace.

Swarthmore College, PA - It's competitive to get in but collaborative once you get there. Achievers will appreciate the elite, rigorous, grad-school readiness nature of the school that is balanced with a supportive and collaborative ethos. This is a college that supports students and their work, which you'll be told all about if you go on a tour and stop to gaze at the giant Adirondack chair designed by a former student.

Claremont Colleges (Scripps, Pitzer, Harvey Mudd, Claremont McKenna, Pomona) - The Claremonts will remind you of a summer camp property, but don't let this mislead you. This family of schools is among the toughest—in admission and curricula—making the consortium very attractive for Achievers. The five-college campus affords students opportunity for collaboration and cross-college learning, so a small college, like Pomona, has the benefits and connections of a larger institution.

Whitman College, WA - This rural school in Walla Walla, Washington makes up for its quiet location with a vibrant and supportive campus community. A leading west-coast liberal arts college, Whitman is less intense and more outdoorsy than some of its east-coast peers. Its slower pace is ideal for Achievers who want rigor, but who don't want all that competitive chaos.

Dartmouth, NH - Known as the Ivy that's made for undergrads, Achievers will find a bit more attention, support, and smaller community in their first four years. Don't think this makes Dartmouth easy to get into or easy to get through (its acceptance rate hovers around 10%). Achievers will find the rigor and prestige they want with the balance they need.

Bangor University, UK - For the student who wants to feel like they are at Oxford (or Hogwarts), Bangor's picturesque campus at the northernmost tip of Wales will offer that ethos of old-world scholarship while still providing a modern, international, and dynamic education.

4.2 THE ARTIST

~~~~~~

You've probably noticed that the acronym STEM (for Science, Technology, Engineering and Math) long considered the holy quaternity of modern education, has recently acquired a new vowel, an A, for "art." I find it wonderfully ironic that progressive education has now entered the age of STEAM. How revolutionary to again appreciate the subject that has been at the core of humanity since drawings in caves were first etched with charcoal!

Thanks to a renewed appreciation for the immense value of great design (see: Apple) art has once again been given a seat at the educational table. And along with art, come artists and iconoclasts.

Similar to *The Geeks Shall Inherit the Earth: Popularity, Quirk Theory, and Why Outsiders Thrive After High School,* by Alexandra Robbins, I'm convinced it will be *artists* (often outsiders) who will inherit the earth.

All labor that's predictable and routine will eventually be automated and performed by robots, leaving humans with the unpredictable, creative, artistic work. Yet, aspiring artists are not encouraged, especially when those creative types dare mention that they want to go to art school. *Gasp!* We all know what will happen to these kids: they'll be living in their parents' basements. I mean, who makes any sort of living after going to *art school?*

Unfortunately, the raw statistics actually don't look great for artists. Parents who Google *highest paying jobs by college major* or *colleges and college majors with the highest ROI* (Return on Investment) will find majors like engineering, computer science, math, and science toward the top of the list. Colleges with the greatest return on investment tend to be those that are strong in these programs, like Harvey Mudd, MIT, and the Colorado School of Mines. The five US Service Academies (Military in West Point, Naval in Annapolis, Air Force in Colorado Springs, Coast Guard in New London, and Merchant Marine in Kings Point) also rate highly, largely because they're mostly free to attend.

The schools with the best ROI are identified by using a combination of 4-year total cost of education, average amount of debt at graduation, years it takes to graduate, the average graduation rate, and 20-year net ROI. (ROI = Difference between 20-Year Median Pay for a bachelor's grad and 24-Year Median Pay for a high school grad minus Total 4 Year Cost.[17]

Sure, typically hard-working students can be found at places like Harvard (along with a few who might be there because of legacy status), and those students will likely continue on to become hard-working adults. Unfortunately, I talk to many highly creative students who would thrive in an art and design college who, because they are good students, are encouraged by parents and teachers to treat art as a hobby but not the main course. What a shame.

When looking at these numbers, it's important to understand the difference between correlation and causation. Majoring in engineering doesn't *cause* you to have a successful, high-paying job out of college, just like going to Harvard doesn't *cause* you to be successful. Sitting at a desk and going through motions won't guarantee anything to anyone.

---

17   https://www.payscale.com/college-roi

It's also important to understand that many students pursue advanced degrees, so their return on their undergraduate investment might not be seen for another 4-8 years down the road, unlike peers who pursue paid work immediately after undergrad. Consider the astrophysicist compared to the civil engineer; the former will likely pursue a PhD, while the latter could easily seek employment directly out of undergrad.

Consider majors like advertising, copywriting, interaction design, graphic design, industrial design, product design, package design, architecture, retail merchandising, and transportation design—all offered at art schools. Who are the designers of our shoes, our cars, our books, our watches, and other consumer goods? Who are the people who work with the engineers, the marketing executives, and the material scientists to make both functional and aesthetic things for everyday life? They are the Creatives.

So why are we often reluctant to support and encourage these types of students? My observation is that, despite our fears, art and design school graduates (or graduates of creative programs at more traditional schools) are some of the best-prepared graduates for today's unpredictable and rapidly changing workforce and economy. Faculty and students at art schools are adopting some pretty innovative practices, perhaps because they have been under scrutiny in the past, but also because of the level of creativity, autonomy, and real-world application they encourage.

Consider the College for Creative Studies in Detroit, where product design students are designing shoes, helmets, crutches, night lights, oil diffusers, furniture, and more. Veronika Scott, an alumna of CCS who, as a student there, invented and designed a coat that could be transformed into a blanket. She got the idea while volunteering with the homeless residents in the area; she saw her product as a way to help. She was beginning to make headway with the design when she was confronted by an angry recipient of her blanket who told her she didn't need a coat, she needed a job.

Veronika is now the CEO and founder of the Empowerment Plan, a nonprofit that employs single parents living in shelters to manufacture that coats that are distributed to help the homeless.

Kirsten was a curious, ambitious, and artistic student who, in high school, got heavily involved in theater set design. Still, she had no idea how her interests could be applied professionally. The daughter of a Danish dad and an American mom, Kirsten had vacationed in Denmark since she was a kid and was convinced that's where she wanted to attend college. Still, she did not know what this would look like or if this was even a feasible option—and she had no idea what she wanted to study, so she didn't know which schools to consider.

When we met, Kirsten told me that she was interested in design; she knew she wanted to pursue something creative. I explained to her that this can mean a lot of things, but she really couldn't go further than that without having a little context. I thought of three people working in different corners of "design" and lined up a few half-day job shadows for her.

Kirsten thought architecture might be a good path, so she shadowed an architect. Next, she shadowed at a luxury office-design firm. Last, she shadowed a young, alternative graphic designer and photographer.

She quickly realized architecture was not for her.

"The field involved much more calculative, on-paper work than I found attractive. I began to seek out careers in design that allowed for more creativity," she told me. With absolute certainty and the confident directness of an informed adult, she told me graphic design was for her; it was a world that seemed to wrap up everything she saw herself doing professionally. She loved the idea of combining graphic arts, technology, and business, and she envisioned herself doing advertising and branding work.

"Within the first few minutes, I knew that this form of design was right up my alley, even if I had little to no experience with art and computer programs," she observed. "What truly appealed to me was the challenge of understanding and connecting with a customer in order to create a product that both fits their needs/desires and defies their imagination."

It didn't take long for her to fall in love with the Copenhagen School of Design (KEA), which has a two-year Business, Technology, and Design program that leads to what's called a "Top-Up Bachelor's Degree." Luckily, Kirsten had attended an IB (International Baccalaureate) school, so her diploma was internationally recognized, making her application a bit easier to complete.

There were still challenges, as when KEA asked for the Danish equivalent of a social security number. It took us a long time to figure out exactly what that was or where to find it. The challenges were made a bit easier, given her dad's Danish background, but Kirsten did not speak Danish, so we had to translate the college website to English, meaning some things got lost in translation (and made for a few humorous situations). Furthermore, unlike US schools, where we can look at the acceptance rates and average test scores and GPA of admitted students, these data were impossible to find at KEA, so we were going on a limb.

To raise the stakes, Kirsten insisted on only applying to KEA, assuring me that if she wasn't admitted, she would take a gap year and reapply. She simply knew she did not want to go to school in the States. "Even though it wasn't clear what I would end up studying, going to Denmark was something anyone close to me knew I wanted, so it never came as a surprise."

As part of her application, Kirsten had to sketch out an advertisement for a fictional men's cologne—an assignment which she knocked out of the park. Fortunately, Kirsten was admitted to KEA, but not until late June, long after her friends made commitments to their respective colleges and universities. I remember at our end-of-year celebration where we mark on a map of the world where everyone will be attending in the fall, Kirsten's push-pin flag had a question mark on it when she stuck it in Denmark on the map.

I interviewed Kirsten at the end of her second year at KEA as she waited to hear back about her acceptance to the Top Up Bachelor's program. She told me that, unlike her friends' college environments, she doesn't really belong to a campus. Instead, she is a resident of Copenhagen.

"My program takes place in just one building nestled in the city, and all of the attending students have completely separate lives outside of the school," she explains.

Naturally, this sort of hands-off, independent college experience isn't for everyone, especially a college freshman from another country! In fact, many US students find themselves unsettled by this kind of learning environment when they go to international schools. But Kirsten was familiar enough with Copenhagen and we talked extensively about the very different college experience she was getting into—she was all about it.

In her first term at KEA, Kirsten found herself "living the dream"—presenting a branding proposal for a new men's clothing line to Denmark's fast-fashion icon, H&M. She is in a Design Student Paradise.

Guiding the Artist

I don't think I'm exaggerating when I say that most students I've worked with are artists in some way. It's just that very few think their *craft* will become anything worth anyone's attention or money.

One thing I suggest to any student who has a creative hobby, whether that's writing poetry, taking photos, doing illustrations in a sketchbook, etc, is to start putting all of it into an online portfolio. Keeping all of their work together may come in handy if, down the road, they decide to apply to a college program that requires a portfolio (majors like graphic design, industrial design, creative writing and advertising often require portfolio submissions).

But there is an advantage for non-design majors, too. Portfolios can be submitted as supplements to college applications as a way of showcasing another side of themselves. I once had a student who was not a prospective art student, but rather a self-described science geek who would come to meetings wearing a faded NASA t-shirt and jeans. She chose to submit a portfolio as a supplement for MIT, which consisted of a series of photos she'd taken to detail the step-by-step process she'd followed to create a Comic-Con costume.

As impractical as it might seem to parents and as worried as they may feel about the idea of their adult kid living in the basement, the creativity of Artist students may actually enable them to ride the waves of economic uncertainty, disruptive change, and unforeseen events throughout their lives. Creativity often comes packaged with resilience, responsiveness, and an original approach to problem solving. Creative students should be supported, encouraged, and shown the myriad doors through which they can walk as Artists.

Tips and Tactics for Supporting the Artist

- Try to appreciate your student's creative stage at this moment without the need to jump into the future and link her present-day passions to future jobs.

- Encourage your Artist to organize her creative work in a portfolio or online website.

- Look for opportunities to introduce your Artist to a wide range of creative professions and introduce him to people who use different forms of creativity every day at work.

- Find ways to supplement your student's school requirements with more creative classes in the community or online.

Sample College List for the Artist

Colleges for Artists should include those schools that are comprehensive schools with strong art programs as well as pure art and design schools. Some Artists might feel better knowing they have a little "wiggle room" and future opportunities to change their minds; for them, schools with more diverse programs (as well as in-depth, hands-on creative programs) will be attractive.

Rochester Institute of Technology - Institutes of technology or polytechnic universities may be the last institutions an artist would consider, but RIT offers some pleasant surprises for the creative types. Digital Imaging Design, Animation and Video Graphics, Game Design, Medical Illustration, Metal and Jewelry Arts, and Furniture Design are just some of the creative—and unique—majors offered at RIT.

College for Creative Studies, MI - Detroit is alive! This is the main message CCS is trying to get out to prospective students; indeed, Detroit is an exciting place for innovative designers who want to design for *change*. The school is very connected to the city, other colleges, and experts from industry. CCS stands out among art schools because of its emphasis on creativity for the greater good. (Remember the student who designed a coat that converts into a blanket, an invention serving the homeless in Detroit during the winter months? This was her school.)

University of Utah - The Multi-Disciplinary Design program at Utah is in a league of its own. Not only is this program unique for a large, public, flagship state school, it is a saving grace for those creatives who just can't quite pin down the creative road they want to choose. Students in the program will explore everything from screen printing to 3D printing, Design Thinking to "Design Ecology," and at the end of it all, they'll earn a BS in Multi-Disciplinary Design.

University of Hawaii, Manoa - An attractive option for anyone, to be sure, this Oahu-based campus is probably not on the radar of most aspiring artists. The University of Hawaii's tuition is less than most art schools; the university also offers steep discounts to students hailing from western states (Western Undergraduate Exchange program). With an innovative Environmental Design program that leads to a Doctorate in Architecture, a major in Apparel Product Design and Merchandising, an Asian Theater Program, and the Theater Design Program, University of Hawaii at Manoa offers some surprising programs (and lots of sunshine).

Copenhagen School of Design (KEA) - KEA could be a great fit for Specialists and for Artists; its super pre-professional curriculum gets students working on industry-relevant projects right away. The school primarily focuses on design disciplines, but also technology and business. Not only will Artists love the colorful and fun city of Copenhagen, but the ability to work on real-world projects adds excitement and energy to the Artist's education.

4.3 THE ADVENTURER

Isabel had an adventurous spirit—and learning style—beginning at a young age. Her parents put her in Montessori school through the primary grades, which was perfect for her. She could explore in a safe space and have enough autonomy and freedom to keep her interests piqued and her mind engaged. But the structure of high school left her feeling in shackles, and she lost motivation. She remembers a select few assignments that allowed her some creative autonomy, like an opinion-piece assignment in one of her English classes that had Isabel up late, putting her all into it. When she was given a little bit of wiggle room, her passions were ignited and motivation was not a problem.

From her new home in British Columbia, I spoke with Isabel over the phone about her journey to a very unconventional, international university.

"You sound so different," I observed. It had been a couple of years since we last spoke. She laughed. Today was her off day and it was 11 AM—practically dawn for a college sophomore. Isabel goes to Quest University, a fairly young, experimental college with about 800 undergraduates. Situated on a hill in picturesque Squamish, BC, just outside of Vancouver, Quest's rainy, serene setting will remind most college-aged students of the cult classic, the *Twilight* series, some of which was actually filmed there. In the winter months, the environment is perfect for curling up in a local coffee shop with a good book.

"I was very unmotivated," Isabel says of her high-school self. Thinking back to the time she dreaded so much, Isabel recalls,

"I was under-challenged but also over-challenged, if that makes sense."

It makes perfect sense. Isabel resisted and despised high school back then, with its busy work, "uninspiring teachers" and religious bias (she attended a private Catholic school in the west and was kicked out of her religion class at least once). She hated all of it and thought college would be more of the same. Isabel remembers thinking there was the Ivy League or her local state school, and nothing in between.

Her brother, Ivy bound from the beginning, had a counselor tell him exactly what he needed to do to get into an Ivy League school. Isabel sat with her brother in the living room as the woman listed the courses he would need to take, the amount of prep he would need to do to get the desired ACT and SAT scores, the extracurriculars he would have to spend time on outside of school, and on and on it went.

Isabel knew right away she wanted none of that. She assumed she was headed for the state school up the road, but that didn't feel good either. She figured she would just have to take advantage of the study abroad program there, be away from campus as much as possible, and try to graduate early.

Isabel's mom echoed this, saying, "She didn't like high school…[she] really hated the whole, 'everybody does x, y, and z.' Isabel's all about what's meaningful."

At Quest, Isabel can be who she has always wanted to be; she no longer feels the pressure to fit into a box.

"Isabel has always been super independent," her mom told me. "[Quest] is certainly supportive of that."

Interestingly, Isabel's mother shared with me that as a kid, her daughter was actually quite shy and attached to mom— very much a homebody. But as Isabel's mom and I talked more, reminiscing about the Isabel of years past, we agreed that while

Isabel is still a bit of a homebody, she can be *at home* anywhere in the world now. She builds roots, develops connections, and gets involved in meaningful ways wherever she is. (Is there such thing as an adventurous homebody? I think we just found one!)

Isabel was the kind of kid who would come home from school, put her homework aside, and read the newspaper or an article about genocide in Myanmar. She was an activist, a culture junkie, and an adventurer at her core. She desperately wanted to study abroad her senior year, but her high school wouldn't accommodate this. She took every opportunity she could to travel, even coming to nanny for my 1-year-old daughter in France while I was doing research there. At one point, she did consider transferring schools and tossed around the idea of homeschooling, but she admits she would have needed a community of peers for homeschooling—or unschooling—to work.

When I asked Isabel's mom if she thought homeschooling would have worked for Isabel, she sort of laughed and moaned at the same time, saying, "Oh my gosh, we would have killed each other."

Isabel's mom also thinks the reason Isabel is doing so well today is the result of *not* being happy in her former learning environment.

"When kids are in a situation they're not really fond of, they look for something different," she says. She believes that the struggle itself was key to Isabel's current success.

Isabel's idea of the best job in the world, back then and still today, was to be a traveling teacher, getting paid to teach around the world. This was one of the signs that suggested Isabel was not lazy or apathetic—she was craving more and high school didn't quench her thirst. A serious risk for students like Isabel is that they'll be labeled as lazy, underachieving, or unambitious because of their grades and test scores. These kinds of kids often fall through the cracks.

"I'm convinced I would have dropped out," was Isabel's response when I asked her where she thinks she'd be today if she'd gone to her state college. Isabel's mom thinks she is more independent, social, and comfortable in her current learning environment; she is more settled in who she is—and who she was all along.

Quest is unique because they employ the "block" schedule, used at a handful of schools in the US, including the more selective Colorado College. This unconventional schedule allows students to choose from a list of courses for each 3.5-week block. Between each block, there is a short break, which allows for a quick trip or some rest. The blocks are intensive but there are no distractions coming from other classes. If you're taking a comparative race and ethnicity class (one of Isabel's favorites so far), that is all you take, every day, for 3.5 weeks.

This allows for Tutors (they're not called professors because professors "profess" their knowledge, while Quest Tutors *facilitate* learning) to take their students on experiential learning adventures to downtown Vancouver—or Rome, if it enhances the learning experience.

"Field Courses" are popular and viable options for students. Some featured field courses include Quest for Antarctica and Visual Anthropology in India. Because of Quest's schedule, the school regularly hosts visiting scholars from around the world who choose to take a month off to come to Quest and host a block course on a topic they find engrossing.

This is what makes the Tutors so engaging and passionate: they are talking about what they really love and care about. Rather than being forced to lecture to an auditorium of hundreds about a broad subject they may or may not personally be invested in, Quest Tutors can offer up course suggestions for each block around specific content they genuinely *want* to talk about! This makes things infinitely more enjoyable for students and Tutors.

And that's why Quest was a perfect fit for Isabel. At Quest, students are asked to pose a question that they want to work to answer by the end of their studies. Together with their advisors, they plan their course schedules in such a way that their questions will be answered by the time they graduate. Isabel is still working on formulating her question, but she said it will have something to do with how best to teach students to be agents of change in the world.

Isabel admits that Quest is not for students who are going to school for a specific job or for students who are getting an education for a specific end. Quest students love the journey; they revel in the process.

Most of Isabel's friends, she told me, will go into nonprofit work, or, if they go on to professional graduate school, they may become human rights lawyers.

"None of my friends here," she says, "will go into consulting or finance."

While Quest is not for everyone, for Isabel, the unique school was the right environment to reignite her passions, foster motivation, and re-discover the curious, deeply engaged person she'd been before her dispiriting slog through high school.

Guiding the Adventurer

Adventurers like Isabel need freedom, autonomy, and an opportunity to explore their surroundings. Many of these students will resist the confines of typical high schools, and if not shown schools like Quest, may choose the path of least resistance or not go to college at all. If adventurers go to traditional high schools with conventions and strict measuring sticks, they may be left feeling deflated and not cut out for college.

It's worth taking your Adventurer to visit some less conventional schools before the light dies out completely; show your student how diverse colleges are and, most importantly, how different from high school they can be. Many students disillusioned by high school may wrongly believe that college is high school on steroids.

Adventurers often resonate with a "hands on" approach to learning and enjoy direct engagement with their subject matter. They learn through experience and utilize all their senses to understand the world.

Consider the schools that emphasize outdoor adventure and exploration as well as a "get your hands dirty" approach to learning, such as Warren Wilson and Sterling Colleges (schools that can also be fits for Skeptics and Independent Learners).

International schools can also be smart options to consider for Adventurers. In addition to Quest in Canada, take a look at the UK schools at UCAS.com or the nearly 1000 programs at German Universities taught in English. You might also consider American universities abroad, such as Franklin University in Switzerland, Bard College Berlin, and the American University of Paris.

Schools like New York University allow students to apply to one of their international schools in Abu Dhabi and Shanghai, in addition to the US-based campus. Block schools, low-residency schools (which allow for ample independent study time), or schools with flexible general education requirements, can be ideal.

Students like Isabel may overlap a bit with the Skeptic and the Independent Learner, who you will meet in later chapters. Isabel shared with me that she probably would have done well as a homeschooled student, if not for the potential isolation that could come with that route. She wanted to be the designer of her own learning environment and of her own curriculum.

If students like Isabel think college will simply be more of what they experienced in high school, they'll either flee or choose the easiest, most convenient route to higher education, just wanting to get it over with. But Isabel was arguably more investigative and inquisitive than most of her peers, so "getting it over with" would have been a tremendous waste, given her talents and interests. She simply needed a place where the adventurer in her could be stimulated while the intellectual in her was nourished.

Tips and Tactics for Supporting the Adventurer

- Help your student see that college can be more of adventure than high school.

- Show your student the study abroad options, international dual-degree options (like the one with The College of William and Mary and St Andrews in Scotland), as well as full degree programs in other countries (NACAC publishes and maintains a guide to admissions at international colleges and universities at nacacnet.org).

- Don't assume (or let your Adventurer assume) that college has to immediately follow high school; explore Gap Year programs together at gapyearassociation.org!

Sample College List for the Adventurer

Adventurers want to see a list of schools that includes colleges that look more exciting than high school, that present new scenery, new people, and new opportunities.

Western Colorado University - With tuition that's hard to beat for out-of-staters, Western is ideal for the Adventurer who doesn't want the added pressure of affording tuition while in college. At Western, Mountaineers get a small-town feel but an "adventure-filled valley," as advertised on the website. With majors in Outdoor Leadership, Environmental Science, Exercise and Sport Science, Geography and Geospatial Analysis, Recreation and Outdoor Education, and Wildlife and Conservation Biology, it's no wonder Western has been ranked one of the most adventurous schools around.

Warren Wilson College, NC - For students who take the phrase, "Get your hands dirty" literally, Warren Wilson could be their idea of heaven. This "work college" requires students to work on campus and do community engagement before they graduate. The campus is supported by a working farm, part of their "1,100-acre classroom." A small, tight-knit community in Asheville, North Carolina, Warren Wilson is surrounded by natural resources that serve as ideal learning environments for Adventurers. Environmental Science, Outdoor Leadership, and Appalachian Studies are all popular majors here.

Minerva University - An experimental university trying to flip conventional instruction methods on their heads, Minerva is based in San Francisco, but very little actually happens there. Students live in 7 different countries throughout their 4 years, taking highly interactive online seminars with renowned professors from around the world. For students who really want to do school in an entirely new way, Minerva could be the perfect fit.

Prescott College, AZ - Prescott might appear to be stuck in the 60s, but this actually adds to its charm and appeal. Attracting students from around the country to the small town of Prescott, AZ, the school has become known as a place for outdoor enthusiasts and those passionate about the environment. Prescott is small—less than 300 students—but this little community is always on the move, incorporating adventure trips into the curriculum. Plan on learning wilderness survival skills, backcountry skiing, and avalanche training.

Quest University, BC, Canada - With just under 1,000 undergraduates, Quest knows exactly the kind of student it wants and students know exactly what kind of school Quest is. Similar to Colorado College with its block schedule (1 course for 3.5 weeks at a time), the curriculum at Quest allows students to go deep in their learning, focusing all of their study efforts on one course at a time. This one-course-at-a-time model is ideal for Adventurers because professors can do local and international field trips with students to enhance the learning experience, not having to worry about interrupting other coursework. Its location in spectacular British Columbia, with mountains, ocean and rivers nearby, also beckons to the Adventurer who loves the outdoors.

4.4 THE SPECIALIST

~~~~~~~~~~~~~~~~~~~~~~~~~~~~~~~~~~

IN THIRD GRADE, LOUISA NEEDED A BOOK TO READ. HER teacher gave her a Nancy Drew book. Louisa rapidly devoured all of the Nancy Drew books. You could probably fill in the rest of this story and it would likely read something like this:

Louisa stayed up all night reading all of the Nancy Drew books, making notes in her diary about the clever tactics, tips, and tricks, mimicking the young detective at school, and asking for spy gear for Christmas.

As cliche as it sounds, this is exactly how Louisa's story unfolded. Louisa knew she wanted to be a sleuth and catch bad guys. It was that simple. As she got older, she refined her objectives and goals, but the general idea stayed the same. She chose sports like martial arts (good for fighting bad guys) and, while other kids were volunteering at the animal shelter, playing soccer, or watching Netflix, she was doing police ride-alongs and shadowing a public defender.

This is rare. While iGeners are career focused, they more often than not have no idea what their specific career will look like (sometimes they'll just pick *something* to be better able to sleep at night). Often, students will begin the college-planning process with an appearance of confidence in their chosen paths, only to choose to cast a slightly wider net before jumping into the depths of post-secondary possibilities.

While many students continue on to college directly after high school to have more time to explore options for their adult lives, students like Louisa don't need to buy time or *figure it out*;

students like Louisa go to college to be professionals-in-training and to prepare for the life they have always known they wanted. While these Specialists may one day change their minds, they will not do so until *they* decide to do so. The best way to support their success: let them do their thing and follow the trail that makes them hungry for more.

Louisa's bright smile, upright posture, and calm demeanor gave the impression that she knew exactly what she was doing today and every day. But despite her resolve, she remained curious, never exuding an ounce of arrogance. Her wide eyes took in everything and she was open to new ideas, but down deep, she knew her chosen path was non-negotiable.

As Louisa navigated her way through high school, she began to see a broader world of possibilities, expanding from a vision of herself as a Nancy Drew-style detective to a lawyer, to an FBI agent, to an Interpol officer. Her self education and independent explorations revealed new and exciting paths within the world of criminal investigation. She considered wider applications of her interests but knew she needed and wanted to begin with the study of criminal justice.

While Louisa considered a number of colleges that had strong criminal justice programs, including American University, Seattle University, George Mason University, and George Washington University, she grew more confident that she wanted to dive into her area of interest right away. She believed that college was her time to become a groomed professional, not necessarily to explore other career options.

When I introduced Louisa to John Jay College of Criminal Justice in the City University of New York system of higher education, she was hooked. It was clear to her that this was her place and those were her people. Many students would hesitate to commit to a college experience as narrowly defined as that offered at John Jay, but Louisa was not nervous at all. She had been utterly committed to and excited about the field from a young age.

Her parents, however, were reluctant. They worried about their oldest daughter going directly to New York City from northern Nevada, unsure if she was prepared for such a transition. They initially urged her to spend two years at a west-coast school and then finish up her education at John Jay. Louisa, however, remained resolute: she convinced them that she would just be wasting time. She was ready to jump in and begin her specialized program of study.

Today, Louisa is in the second half of her first year at John Jay. She has no regrets. While many out-of-state students might feel out of place in this commuter school, where many students are locals and go home on the weekends, Louisa says the trade-off is worth it. She loves that every class, even her general education classes, has a focus on justice, especially international justice.

She has taken a course on Sex Crime and Trafficking, and another one called International Criminal Justice. Her Freshman Seminar topic was Latino Justice Studies and her English class is learning about child soldiers in Liberia. Her classes are small, her peers are all on similar paths and have similar career-mindedness, and she has regular contact with professionals in the field, even getting a chance to visit their work spaces to experience the full flavor of their careers.

Louisa is absolutely in her element. She told me she "was never nervous about going to such a specialized school," adding, "I was always so committed to the field." For her, criminal justice is a *calling*.

Guiding the Specialist

Many career-centric Specialists enjoy looking at international schools, especially in Europe and Canada, because they generally eschew the extensive general education courses required in the liberal arts curricula at US colleges. The latter, in fact, are ideal for students who are still exploring—or who *say* they know what they want to do, but may really have no idea.

The kind of exploration and interdisciplinary approach that liberal arts colleges excel at can be great for the Specialist who still desires a broad-based education. Don't rule these schools out, even if you're working with a student like Louisa. Kirsten, who you met in the Artist chapter, is similar to Louisa. She knew she wanted to study graphic design and knew she wanted to be in Denmark, where she held citizenship. Her program is a highly specialized, career-oriented design program.

I'm usually the proponent of casting a wide net, starting broad and gradually getting more specialized, while keeping options open. This approach works for many students. But I've also learned to support the student who displays intense interest in something, even if it seems unrealistic or pie-in-the-sky. That unique intensity provides motivation to help them push through obstacles.

It's important to determine if the would-be Specialist student's interest is deep rooted, or if they're simply coming up with an answer to the inevitable question, "What do you want to do?" Asking teens what they want to be when they grow up is a major source of stress, and guaranteed to provoke eye rolling. Getting an adult off their backs with a palatable answer is a common stratagem.

It may work better to ask what they would like to *try* rather than commit to, long term. For example, "What would you think about trying this space camp?" or "How does this art class sound to you?" would likely meet with a better response than, "What do you want to be when you grow up?" or "What are you going to major in?"

Once that *Thing* is discovered, let them run with it and step out of the way (except maybe to pay for said Thing—yes, parents, you still have a role!)

After watching the musical *The Greatest Showman*, my 4-year-old daughter was a trapeze artist. Our TRX straps (you know, those work-out straps that dangle from the ceiling, calling you to do your body-weight-resistance routine—a call you ignore most days) became her trapeze. She would swing into things and hop off, stumbling before she straightened up, hands raised, eyes closed, waiting for the applause.

This became a source of great comedic entertainment for my husband and me, but I didn't think much of it. Until I discovered Circus Arts. Did you know such a thing existed? In Chicago, there is not just one, but multiple Circus Arts facilities that offer classes and camps for kids. I signed our daughter up for a one-week camp, expecting she would probably lose interest by the end, much like she has with other activities, but to our surprise and delight, she asked, "Can I do circus camp for a million years?" and "Can I go there instead of school?"

We're still debating the last one, but we told her, "Yes, you can do this as long as you want."

On her own, Louisa sought out a ride along with her uncle who was a police officer and a job shadow with a friend's mom, a public defender. This didn't take any pushing or prodding, and Louisa genuinely enjoyed these experiences.

If your student isn't coming up with such opportunities on his or her own, it may be helpful to present some. You may

91

also want to make an introduction to facilitate that exploration. Young people, even motivated ones, can be shy and awkward when approaching adults in jobs they admire. But if your student doesn't respond with some kind of forward momentum, let it go and move on to something else. If you push him too hard down any one path, he will either grow to resent that path or come to believe that this path is the only path you'll be pleased to see him follow.

For the majority of Specialist students, a highly specialized program at a commuter campus where they're not locals won't be an ideal fit. Not many Specialists, even motivated ones, possess the maturity and self confidence to thrive in such an independent environment. However, for the right student, it's important to not rule out this type of school. Louisa not only found a great college "fit," but an affordable one as well, with tuition far lower than the other schools she considered.

Tips and Tactics for Supporting the Specialist

- Know when to step back and let the Specialists go deep in their "thing" and discover *by doing* if that really is the right path for them.

- Help your Specialist find mentors who do what they're interested in doing and try to set up job shadows with these professionals. Encourage the student to keep a journal; this is a great way to refer back to experiences.

- If you find that your students are linking to a specialization because they want a quick response to those nagging questions about what they will be when they grow up, well, then stop asking those nagging questions.

Sample College List for the Specialist

Specialists appreciate specific, career-oriented studies, but it's important to respect and plan for future changes and "pivots." Colleges that have specialized areas of study along with broader programs, are nice compliments to those highly focused and technical schools. Comprehensive universities that offer associates degrees or specialized certificates can also be great fits for these students.

Since Specialists are so, well, specialized, I'm including examples of some colleges that offer career-oriented majors and narrow specializations for a variety of Specialists.

Cooper Union for the Advancement of Science and Art, NY - previously free to all students who could get into this competitive institution in New York City, Cooper Union has since introduced a tuition rate that is about $22,000 per year (less than most private institutions in the US). The Cooper Union campus is less a campus and more a modern makerspace. One giant main building houses rows of messy rooms where some students sit and listen, but most do. You can only get three degrees at this school: a Bachelor of Fine Arts, a Bachelor of Architecture, and a Bachelor of Engineering, so Specialists can rest assured knowing that they will be in good company with their narrowly-focused peers. But don't be alarmed by the limited degree offerings; Cooper Union still requires students to take a broad range of courses in the Humanities and Social Sciences.

California Polytechnic University, San Luis Obispo, CA - Aside from being a school that emphasizes science and technology, with particularly strong programs in agricultural sciences, Cal Poly also wants students to choose their area of study at the time they apply. This might scare away those students still in exploration mode, but Specialists will cherish the opportunity to get to work in their chosen field as soon as possible. Cal Poly's hands-on, experiential teaching methods connect students to the real-worldliness of their chosen majors.

Colorado School of Mines, CO - While suitable for students who don't aim to be mining professionals, this school offers majors that will best prepare students for careers in mining and related fields, whether that be Petroleum Engineering or Geophysics and Seismology. School of Mines is a medium-sized school with just under 5,000 undergraduates, the majority of whom are men (a rarity at US colleges today).

CUNY John Jay College of Criminal Justice, NY - Part of the City University of New York college system, John Jay offers a more affordable option for those Specialists who know that the world of Criminal Justice is where they want to be. At John Jay, criminal justice expands to include things like Securities Services, Fire Science and Prevention, Forensic Science and Technology, and Legal Studies. Specialists can get even more specialized than they thought possible and really dive in to become true experts in their chosen fields. Students will gain lots of professional connections through internships and site visits during their time at John Jay.

Babson College, MA - Whether you have been told you will take over your parents' business since the time you could walk, or you can't ever imagine yourself working for a "boss," Babson is for the Specialists who see no other option than to study business and entrepreneurship. Every student at Babson is studying some aspect of business and many students launch businesses during their undergrad years (there is even seed funding for some lucky students). If you are considering Babson, make sure you can handle the intensity by checking out their summer program for high school students: Introduction to the Entrepreneurial Experience.

LONG AFTER IT'S NO LONGER ACCEPTABLE TO DRESS UP AS Superman and Wonder Woman, some students still yearn to be the rescuers, the protectors, the defenders of good, and the fighters of evil. The Hero is that student who feels compelled to go into some sort of public service. This includes students who are interested in law enforcement, like the Specialist we featured earlier, as well as firefighting, the military, and public office.

These students tend to be fairly conventional; they are at their happiest and most effective with order and guidelines. "Conventional" students, according to the YouScience assessment, are those who have a preference for work and activities with a good amount of structure, rules, and order.

Careers that are high on the Conventional interest scale include law enforcement, criminal investigation and forensic science, technicians, accounting, carpentry, and some engineering professions. If you combine the Realistic and Conventional interest types, you get someone who is attracted to work that is hands on or physical—often outdoors—and that offers clear objectives and tangible results. They are comfortable with a hierarchy, or chain of command, and prefer to be part of a team. These are not the students who color outside the lines, but the ones who ensure that the lines are clear, accurate, and well maintained.

I've had my own stereotypes about Heroes challenged in my work. I have seen my fair share of that stereotypical Hero—the classic example being the rural, conservative kid who's wowed by the military recruiters at his high school and enlists before high-school graduation.

But I have also seen the very opposite: the Big Mountain ski bum with a liberal, laid-back persona who applies to and is accepted by the Air Force Academy.

In my experience, there are common features among these students. They are almost always absolutely certain about their future goals and will rarely consider alternatives to this goal. For example, my students who apply to the military academies may apply to a couple of "back-up" schools, but they do so grudgingly. They feel "called" or compelled to go into service; they tend to be good students, but may not *love* high school or the typical achievement benchmarks set up in high school. They are a devoted bunch with laser focus, which can be mis-understood (or, perhaps, correctly understood) as stubbornness.

Some parents, especially when there is no history of service in the family, have a difficult time understanding their student's sense of devotion. For the dyed-in-the-wool Hero, the call to serve seems to be something innate—though it's not always something they can articulate.

I once asked a student about his decision to join the Army. He replied reflexively, "I don't know. That's just what I think I have a duty to do." Without exactly saying it, he let me know that, while I might not understand, it's entirely normal to answer the call of duty.

One of the most important pieces of advice I can offer when working with these students is to provide them early exposure to people working in their area of interest. Some students are, understandably, drawn in by the exciting depictions of military, law enforcement, and firefighting that they see in movies, TV shows, and increasingly realistic video games. Exposure to these actual careers can offer a reality check, especially if no one in their family works in this space.

Some students have very unrealistic notions about what the Air Force Academy, for example, is really like, or what a 4-year commitment to serve actually means. Some students may simply feel the need to prove themselves, and to demonstrate their strength, grit, and perseverance. This can sometimes be a reaction to a family environment in which those qualities are conspicuously absent.

The same young man who reflexively recited his call to serve, insisted on a military career with robotic certainty. Recognizing no suitable alternatives to military life, he numbly recited to me the reasons for "choosing" this path: duty, responsibility, obligation. His flat affect bordered on disturbing, and only later did I learn that this boy came from an abusive family, and one where he had assumed the role of caregiver for his disabled brother. Duty, responsibility, and obligation were all he knew.

Still, many Heroes will go into a branch of the military after seeing a relative do the same. In 2016, a *Time Magazine* report on Pentagon data showed that "80% of recent troops come from a family where at least one parent, grandparent, aunt or uncle, sibling or cousin has also worn their nation's uniform. More than 25% have a parent who has served."[18]

But these numbers don't tell us the whole story. While I've worked with students who looked to the military as a viable career option, those numbers are actually down. According to a Politico article by John Spencer, "The number of Americans eligible to serve in the military is dramatically shrinking, leaving the Army at its smallest size in over 75 years and forcing units to rely on unstable and unprepared servicemen."

---

18   http://time.com/4254696/military-family-business/

Perhaps the reason I've seen so many students interested in this path is because I did a great deal of work in rural schools, where military recruiters seem to be a permanent installation. It's not hard to understand the appeal of "getting out" of communities where populations are dwindling and local businesses closing, reducing opportunity. But students in other parts of the country are opting more and more for non-military educational paths.

In one of the most revealing articles on the topic, "The Ivy League Was Another Planet," published in the *New York Times* in March of 2013, Claire Vaye Watkins talks about growing up in rural Nevada, where military recruiters were far more familiar than college recruiters. Not only could her friends not become familiar with elite colleges, but those colleges could not become familiar with the students, either.

"I never saw a college rep at Pahrump Valley High," she writes, "but the military made sure that a stream of alumni flooded back to our school in their uniforms and fresh flat-tops, urging their old chums to enlist."

Despite the disproportionate numbers of rural students enlisting, the military is still not seeing the numbers of new recruits they expected to see after eliminating the draft.

"The government's current difficulty in assembling a full force dates to 1973, when the United States eliminated the draft and transitioned into an all-volunteer system," writes John Spencer in a 2015 *Politico* piece. "The major assumption undergirding that move was a belief that Americans would volunteer for military service when national security is at risk. But the past 14 years of war have proven that that assumption is wrong."[19]

---

19 https://www.politico.com/agenda/the-militarys-real-problem-fewer-americans-are-joining-000005

The idea of using military service as a launch pad for education has become an increasingly risky strategy for would-be college students of all ages. Fewer troops and a constant state of war since 9/11 have resulted in longer deployments and more service members leaving with disabilities. These outcomes have made it harder to get this strategy to work to a student's advantage.

Brooke saw her brother join the Air National Guard after high school and was fairly certain she'd follow in his footsteps: she'd attend her local state university while she did her mandatory training, one weekend per month. Brooke did entertain other possibilities for college, and applied to a few out-of-state schools. But in the end, joining the Guard provided her with the financial resources, as well as the sense of belonging and purpose she needed. She opted for the local university.

I interviewed Brooke just after she completed boot camp in Texas and as she was beginning Tech School in Virginia, where, she said, she was "learning about the job I'll be doing while at the Guard."

Brooke described boot camp to me in an email:

> Boot camp was extremely intense the first two weeks; it was constant yelling, marching, immunizations, and being on my feet. You learn very quickly all about time management, attention to detail, and how to keep your "military bearing." Military bearing is being able to maintain your bearing, no matter what's going on around you, not laughing, or even smirking. The core values are also instilled into you very early on, they consist of: Integrity first, Service before self, and Excellence in all we do. Learning to always do the right thing no matter what.

Brooke was not discouraged by the initial challenges she faced. "Community," "belonging," "usefulness," and "purpose" are among the benefits most frequently mentioned by students who go into service.

"Being involved with the Guard makes me enjoy being around people a lot more," Brooke told me. "I've met so many new people and experienced so many new things. I really enjoy being around people that share similar goals with me."

While it's surprising to many parents of teens, it's common for students to talk about the structures and conventions evident in service domains like the military, to be absolute positives.

"(The) Military lifestyle is mature and very well organized," Brooke enthused. "I've become so used to my everyday routine and have actually started enjoying myself."

College was still very much a part of Brooke's plans, but she decided to put it off for a year in order to get boot camp and Tech School out of the way before she started. It's possible to start college the fall after high school graduation, but it can be tricky to carve out the time for these initial steps. However, once those initial pieces are complete, college and the National Guard can go nicely together.

Some students only join the Guard for the tuition benefits, but sometimes, like Brooke, they end up liking it more than they thought.

"I plan on going to college and still continuing to work at my Guard base. I'll be able to attend classes as usual, and work my one weekend a month at the base. We also have to work two weeks a year, which I could do during my off time in the summer," she told me. "I've also considered going through college, obtaining my bachelor's degree, then re-enlisting through my contract and going from Guard to active—then I would be able to commission as an officer!"

The Guard does a good job of outlining college and career paths for students in a clear, linear way. This can be very reassuring for students who feel lost and want to have a plan.

On its website, the Guard lists a variety of career options students can pursue, including Paralegal Specialist, Army Band Musician, Chaplain Assistant, and Electronic Warfare Specialist (imagine this guy at career day). By clicking on one of those career options, students get a detailed description of not only what that Guard career path looks like, but what the same career path could look like in civilian life.

Students can then view a detailed Career Timeline, outlining the steps they would need to take in and outside of the Guard, and showing the many options and opportunities to "stack" credentials. Like Brooke, many students find great comfort in knowing how their experiences stack on top of each other, and that every step they take is moving them toward a clear goal. This is obviously not something available to students in the conventional educational system—and it's easy to see why it would be appealing to those who appreciate order and certainty.

Another student, Miles, attends the Air Force Academy in Colorado. When I managed to catch up with this busy young man, he told me about "Recognition," an initiation he'd just finished.

This, he explained, is "basically three days where the freshmen just get screamed at. Most fun I never want to have again." He went on to say, "So life is pretty good now. It's a grind here, but I love it and am doing better than I expected."

When we first met, Miles was a competitive Free Ride or "big mountain" skier in high school. This brand of no-rules, no-goals, anything-goes backcountry skiing is high-risk and exhilarating to watch. The athletes who gravitate to this sport are the same people who jump out of planes, fly off of bridges in squirrel suits, and generally embrace activities with a high probability of injury or fatality.

At first, I'd been surprised that this laid-back "ski bum" was set on joining the Airforce, but in retrospect, it makes perfect sense. Miles wanted not only his activities, but eventually his job, to offer the risk and adrenaline he craved. He wanted every aspect of his life to be action packed, but more than that, he wanted his life and career to offer satisfaction, reward, and a great sense of purpose.

I asked Miles to explain his attraction to the military.

"I always felt a certain obligation to serve, so that almost wasn't even a decision for me. The decision was choosing how I was going to serve," he replied. "I naturally gravitate toward more adrenaline-filled activities, and this projected my interest in flying and attending the Academy. For me, serving was inevitable—the risk and excitement is just an added bonus."

For being an intense, risk-seeking kid, Miles was a surprising realist who thought pragmatically and followed the numbers. He was the kind of kid who, after rigorous calculations, determined the minimal amount of effort he needed to put forth in order to maintain good grades. It worked. He ended up graduating in the top 10% of his class with a 4.07 GPA.

For most of his high-school years, Miles thought he would pursue a career in skiing. As time went on, though, and despite his skill level, he realized he didn't have the passion required for that path. He began to think about something he'd always secretly wanted to pursue.

"I've always had a deep fascination and respect for the military," he told me. "I think, deep down, I always wanted to be in the military, but throughout my life, no one I knew was very supportive of the idea so I didn't consider it. When I began to sit down and think about what I really wanted to do with my life, being in the military was the only thought present."

"So I planned on enlisting in the military," he continued, "but my friends and family convinced me to apply to the Air Force Academy."

Miles has never regretted his decision to go to the US Air Force Academy, but the environment—and the application process—is not for the faint of heart. Miles shared with me that at one time or another, usually during freshman year, most students will question who they are and what they are doing there.

Unless a student is absolutely dead set on a specific branch of the military, Miles recommends visiting all of the Military Academies before applying. This provides a better understanding of the different branches and what to expect. That tour would include the United States Military Academy (West Point), the Naval Academy, the Air Force Academy, the Coast Guard Academy, and even the Merchant Marine Academy.

The Military Academies are not just tough to survive, they are tough to get into. The current admissions rate at the USAFA hovers around 12%. The process to apply begins much earlier than that of traditional schools, usually around spring of junior year. I tell students that applying to an Academy requires several applications within an application. Students must secure congressional, senatorial, or vice-presidential nominations, pass a fitness assessment and character assessment, submit a medical evaluation, and complete the school's actual application.

Miles recalls the most challenging part being the nominations.

"You're competing in your district or state for a very valuable appointment, and the nomination-application process is almost as demanding as the whole application to the Academy," he told me. "And as most can relate, waiting to hear if you were accepted is one of the more taxing challenges."

And after all of that, you may not get in. Then what? Good thing Heroes are determined, or stubborn, depending on how you look at it. These aren't the kids who are willing to settle for any alternative. Some students will take a year off and reapply, go into an ROTC program at a traditional college, or enlist directly in the military.

Miles knew he wasn't quite ready to apply to the Academy, so immediately after high school, he attended a semester-long program at Northwestern Preparatory School. This school in the San Bernardino Mountains is ideal for students who aren't admitted or aren't ready to apply to one of the Academies. It provides preparatory coursework and a residential experience, as well as an introduction to military life and what to expect at the Academies. After Miles finished the fall semester at NWP, he took some additional courses at a college near his home, in order to get some introductory college courses under his belt. While at NWP, he received support preparing his application and securing his nominations to apply to the Air Force Academy.

Miles, like Brooke, tells me the personal development and the bonds forged are among the most rewarding aspects of the Academy. Miles is in his element and doing what he always pictured himself doing, even though it wasn't popular among his circle of friends and family. When I asked him what he thinks the future holds, he responded, "As of now, I am still very intent on becoming a pilot, which has a service commitment of 10 years after receiving your pilot wings. As of now, I plan on going career and serving 20 years, but it's difficult to say what the future holds."

Guiding the Hero

Heroes want to be treated as independent, self-sufficient adults—even if their parents and guides don't yet see them that way. Though you may not believe that the military, for example, is best for your son or daughter, try exploring the options with them and help them meet people who have experience in this domain. You might be surprised by how many options there are for your student.

I recommend looking not only at the Federal Service Academies (US Air Force Academy, US Military Academy, US Naval Academy, US Merchant Marine Academy, and US Coast Guard Academy), but also the National Guard and ROTC programs at traditional colleges.

It's also possible to send your aspiring military recruit to summer exposure programs or a pre-academy prep school, like the one that Miles attended after high school. Students can also try to attend military prep high schools. These can be private, such as the Army and Navy Academy in Carlsbad, California, or public, such as the Air Force Academy High School in Chicago, Illinois. Such experiences will definitely take your student beyond the glamour of recruiting ads and provide a taste of what military life is really like.

For students who think they want to go into law enforcement or investigation (at local, national, or international levels) majors in criminal justice or criminology might be obvious choices, but not the only ones. Someone who aspires to work at the FBI, for example, will find that an array of degrees beyond criminal justice can serve as their launch pad, while keeping a wide number of career options open. Degrees in business, accounting, computer science, cybersecurity, finance, economics, law, and political science are desirable for aspiring special agents, as are science degrees, including physics, biology, and chemistry. Law degrees and accounting degrees are among the FBI's most sought-after qualifications.

Language-loving Heroes can gain a degree in one or more languages to become an FBI linguist or interpreter. A degree in Spanish, Russian, Chinese, Vietnamese, or Arabic would position your Hero to work in law enforcement or other intelligence services. A B.A. and three years of work experience, or an advanced degree and two years of work experience, will generally be needed for an FBI job.

Not surprisingly, a Hero interested in a career with the CIA may choose to study criminal justice or criminology, but degrees in sociology and psychology are also popular on this path. As with the FBI, language and science degrees are desirable too.

Becoming a Foreign Service Officer (FSO) is another potential career path for Heroes. The State Department offers five distinct career tracks. To provide a better idea of what such careers entail, there are multiple internship programs offered, both domestically and internationally. Per the State Department website, they're looking for "diverse, culturally aware, well-rounded and strategic problem-solvers," for their internships. The Pathways program, which offers paid domestic internships, has opportunities for high school and college students alike.

https://careers.state.gov/intern/student-programs/

You can also help your Hero student gain exposure to a wider variety of service paths, including diplomacy, education, non-profit work, and political/advocacy work.

Let us not forget about another kind of service that will resonate with the Heroes: volunteerism. Options include the Peace Corps, Americorps, City Year, Teach for America, and ServiceCorps. At home or abroad, Heroes seek purpose, even if that means forgoing a traditional job or the path to profit.

Fortunately, many service programs, such as those mentioned above, offer benefits ranging from stipends to student loan repayment assistance.

One important role you serve as a guide in this process is a filter and a balancing force for your student. For example, if your Hero seeks adrenaline highs, adventure, and risk, the language on military websites can be tantalizing. Take this excerpt from the National Guard website:

> Nothing compares to the rush you feel rappelling from an Army assault helicopter. Learn to maximize the use of these million-dollar aircraft during training and combat.[20]

Heck, this kind of language makes *me* excited! You can imagine how a young person, seeking an escape from the mundane routines of high-school life, would be drawn to this. It sounds like a game. Your job is to help your student understand the reality of such paths, not to discourage them altogether.

The superhero in your student may not need the Air Force Academy or the National Guard to be fully expressed, but for the two students in this chapter, it was how they found their people, their challenge, and their element. They stepped into service for their country and into the leadership and purpose they craved.

---

20   https://www.nationalguard.com/

Tips and Tactics for Supporting the Hero

- Offer an outside perspective, ideally with the help of people who possess direct experience.

- Help your student see through language that may not present the whole truth or that might be hyperbolic.

- Shed some light without blinding your kid in the process. If your kid feels like you are trying to persuade him away from the military, for example, he may feel that much more compelled to pursue it. Share the wide array of career and education paths that could resonate with the heroic sensibility.

- Remember that Heroes can find the service and the purpose they crave in a variety of roles; you can help by exposing them to some of the roles Heroes can fill.

Sample College List for the Hero

Aside from Military academies and schools for criminal justice, Heroes can excel in a number of schools that have a strong focus on social justice, global impact, learning for purpose, and camaraderie. Some of these schools are ideal for Heroes who are also Specialists, because of the narrow focus of study, but others might seem like good fits for those Heroes who may have a little Adventurer in them.

Embry Riddle Aeronautical University, AZ & FL - Akin to a military base, Embry Riddle was made for those students who like the idea of military service but aren't quite ready for the commitment. More specifically, it is made for students who want to fly. Not only do several students take flight lessons here, but the library itself is designed to look like a runway. As my tour guide told me when I visited the Arizona campus, "Students here can't help but stare everytime a plane flies overhead," which they do pretty regularly. Students can study anything from Aeronautical Engineering to International Relations, and their top-notch facilities allow students to conduct experiments to learn things like the greatest wind pressure that a certain airplane siding can withstand, and to experience a realistic air-traffic-control simulation.

The Federal Service Academies (US Air Force Academy, US Military Academy, US Naval Academy, US Merchant Marine Academy, and US Coast Guard Academy) - If you can get through the multi-step application process for the Service Academies, which includes a Congressional nomination, a fitness test, and essays, you will be rewarded with a tuition-free college education (if you don't count the commitment to serve after graduation, usually a five-year commitment).

George Washington University, D.C - George Washington has an obvious focus on government, politics, and foreign service. For students who want to serve in ways that don't necessarily require bootcamp and weapons training, George Washington can be a good option. Located in D.C., students have easy access to a variety of opportunities to link them to their future service-oriented professions, whether that's in politics, diplomacy, or criminal justice; it's no wonder GW is a national leader when it comes to internships for students.

Washington and Lee University, VA - The Shepherd program for Poverty Studies and Mudd Center for Ethics are two of the programs of interest for Heroes. Shepherd offers a minor called "Interdisciplinary Study of Poverty and Human Capability," which requires courses in economics, education, law, philosophy, politics, sociology, and more, along with service and internship opportunities. The Mudd Center reaches across the entire university to promote greater dialogues, teaching, and research around public and professional ethics issues. Students who have a serious commitment to social justice, equality, and activism will find a home at Washington and Lee.

Texas A&M University - Not only does it have a School of Military Science, Texas A&M was also ranked as one of the best schools for veterans by Collegechoice.net. Students can minor in Military Studies and take courses in Aerospace Studies, Military Science, and Naval Science. The School of Military Science also offers a certificate in Leadership Study and Development. Other than academics, Heroes will find a huge, spirited campus in Texas A&M, with no shortage of majors, programs, clubs, or sports.

4.6 THE SKEPTIC

ANDY RECENTLY INTERNED FOR TWO MONTHS IN NEPAL with an organization, started by a friend, that builds and maintains schools. He's leaving soon for a trip to Senegal, where he'll be taking classes at a university and doing an internship. Andy is studying Social and Behavioral sciences at Soka University in southern California. In a recent conversation, he told me, "All of my friends are international…my girlfriend is Japanese. I've learned so much about what's going on around the globe." Yet he recalls, "I was so skeptical about Soka before I came here."

Andy was not excited about college. Not even a little.

"Why are we doing this?" I would ask myself, as I sat awkwardly with him in the downtown coworking space where I first started working with students.

Andy was one of my first student clients. He would come to our meetings and leave them absolutely unaffected by anything I said, presented, or suggested. In fact, he displayed the best example of a "flat affect" that I'd ever seen. I sometimes wondered if he might fall asleep right in front of me.

But Andy was smart, observant, and witty; he also had been diagnosed with mild autism. His skepticism about college could easily have been interpreted as laziness. Andy was smart in some traditional ways—he earned 4s and 5s on his AP exams—and also in some less conventional ways—he started a club at his school called the "House of Discussion" where meaningful debate and dialogue could happen in a civil fashion. He was interested in history and enjoyed writing fairy tales. He aspired to become a botanist, loved spending time outdoors, and sometimes volunteered as a clean river monitor.

He also cared deeply about his classmates, volunteering as a peer mentor for students with learning and developmental differences. He lost his best friend in high school—a quick and unexpected death—which made him feel even closer to his remaining peer group.

But there was also a shadow that hung over him and it made him cynical, skeptical, and terribly sad. He wanted to stay close to home, admitting that he wanted to remain near his mom. Andy's disinterest in continuing his education made his mom nervous. She knew how much he needed to grow and that this growth had to happen away from home.

Andy's dad was frustrated with his son's apparent lack of motivation, and let it be known that he wouldn't invest anything in post-secondary schooling if his son wasn't going to take it seriously. Andy's parents were also concerned about his future employment prospects. Because of Andy's autism, his parents always wondered what "adulting" would look like for him. I understood why his dad thought that getting Andy to complete a career-focused, two-year degree was the smartest thing to do at the time.

Andy was uninterested in the overall chaos, competitiveness, and vulnerability in college admissions, which, I imagine in retrospect, appeared grossly superficial to him. He was not uninterested because he didn't know what was going on; he was uninterested because he truly believed this whole college thing was not for him.

After some time, and several conversations about different colleges, it became clear that Andy's lack of interest was in part due to his misapprehension about colleges. He thought that every college was huge, with big Greek life, lots of parties, and giant lecture halls. I realized that Andy wanted a smaller school with independent learners, an emphasis on social justice and global impact, opportunities to get out of the classroom, and to be surrounded by deep thinkers. He needed to see the less conventional side of higher education; he needed to see students like him thriving in schools that were nothing like the schools he knew.

First, I'll say that Andy was admitted to all of the schools to which he applied. While he was excited about his offers, he was still apprehensive about the idea of leaving home. That is, until he visited Soka University.

Soka is a small gem of a school in Aliso Viejo, in southern California. Rooted in the belief that an education should focus on bettering humanity, and with a diehard focus on international competence and understanding, Soka is truly something unique. It is highly ranked among liberal arts schools and even considered a "Best Value" in the *US News and World Report* rankings.

With an average class size of 12, many students will claim Soka it is too small for their liking, but with a student body comprising 40% international students and many opportunities for study abroad, the Soka experience is anything but limited and dull.

Andy first visited Soka during a trip to southern California for a fencing tournament. He later did an overnight visit, which I strongly recommend whenever possible. During that trip, he was sold on the academics there—a unique, interdisciplinary curriculum that emphasizes international competence in a small, caring, and compassionate community.

In a recent conversation, Andy's mom told me about the talk they had on a bench on Soka's campus, shortly after the tour. She told me they both knew, instantly, that this school was different. Not just because it was a small liberal arts school (there were other such schools that Andy did not like) but because it felt so intentional, compassionate, and international. Indeed, Soka's mission is to "foster a steady stream of global citizens committed to living a contributive life."

Andy's mom has seen a dramatic transformation in her son, one that she does not think would have occurred had he been allowed to have it his way and go to the safe-feeling, nearby state school.

"Parents have to be willing to take a risk," she told me. "We told Andy that if he didn't engage, he would have to come home."

His mom sent me this email after his first semester there:

Soka was the perfect place for Andy—he is a different person!

- He has made so many friends from so many parts of the world and he loves the size of Soka because you get to know everyone and you see them all everyday
- He is totally taken with a girl!
- He signed up for 5 classes and is doing really well, he also completed a 3 credit course over the summer
- He joined 3 clubs (Kendo, traditional Indian dance, and Charity-in-Action)
- He volunteered to help at a fundraiser for Nepal and at the Peace Gala
- He doesn't let me get involved in anything—he handles everything himself
- He hasn't played World of Warcraft since he left home
- When I text him to check in, he texts back "Don't worry, I'm thriving."

"While he still doesn't know what he wants to do [for a career], we are definitely less concerned about it now," his mom told me. She and her husband now see motivation and enthusiasm in their son, and know these qualities will enable him to be successful at whatever he decides to do. They are confident now that he will figure it out, put himself out there, and show up.

This sort of success story is what makes my job so enjoyable. Andy's advice to current high-school students who are Skeptics?

"Go check it out."

Guiding the Skeptic

It's all too common to hear parents say they refuse to spend any money on their "unmotivated" kids. While money alone certainly won't motivate a teenager (well, maybe money paid directly to a teen will do the trick!) it will often take an investment of time, money, or both to inspire someone who is having an especially difficult time finding his groove. It's difficult not to make comparisons between such kids and the "born-motivated" variety, and presume that the latter are the only ones worthy of investment.

An unmotivated, "stuck" teen rarely becomes motivated if there's no change in their environment or involvement in new activities. Unfortunately, this is what many frustrated parents expect, and it causes a lot of anger and disappointment. While I sympathize with parents who feel they've already wasted enough money on an unmotivated kid and can't justify wasting more on college, it's a mistake to assume that this student should just "get college over with" in the cheapest, fastest way possible.

The failure of imagination around college is not limited to students like Andy. Even parents who have attended college themselves usually refer exclusively to their own, limited experiences when trying to understand if their student is "college material." There is different "material" required for every college, and there are many, many colleges out there.

It may even be wrong to assume your teen is actually "unmotivated." He may just be *uninterested* in his present options, like Andy was. Stepping away from the Cult of College Prestige will likely be the first step to take with a Skeptic.

He may also be having a hard time focusing on the future and seeing later payoffs for current efforts. Perhaps your kid is more "present focused" than "future focused." Each type has its positives and negatives (and I advise focusing on the positives!)

I once had a student who was very much a present focuser. He was really good at making the most of the present moment, completing things that were staring him in the face, and living each day like it would be his last. This part of his personality made sense; he had lost his dad to cancer when he was about 12 years old, and I imagine he'd learned a thing or two about seizing the day. Still, college planning—and any kind of future planning—was a challenge for him.

When it was time to write his college essays, I encouraged him to focus on this personality trait, which he'd always thought was a disadvantage. So he wrote an essay that observed how kids who can plan for the future are the ones who are rewarded in high school—but that this was not him. He wrote about being the kind of kid who is present, who stops and smells the roses, and who lives each day fully.

Andy's mom recognized his potential and his creativity, describing him as "an ember that could take fire in the right environment." In high school, Andy was spending a lot of time in his room, not socializing and not showing much interest in anything.

Left to their own devices, many Skeptics get stuck and stay stuck, preferring their "comfort zone" to the myriad uncertainties of the world. Because they can be stubborn and unresponsive, some parents tire of trying to interest their Skeptics in anything. A local college may be wholly uninspiring to the Skeptic, but it ticks the "college" box for the family. The Skeptic may muddle through, or even fail, in such an environment, reinforcing the parents' belief that they were not worth a bigger investment. The Skeptic too has their worst fears reinforced, unaware that they could have had an exciting and fulfilling college experience somewhere else.

When it comes down to it, students and families often "don't know what they don't know."

Tips and Tactics for
Supporting the Skeptic

- Present him with options he hasn't considered, and demonstrate that not all schools fit his stereotype. This can help him become more willing to consider new ideas.

- Stick with it! Skepticism can be de-motivating and de-energizing for the people around the Skeptic. Recognize that helping Skeptics takes energy and patience.

- Get your Skeptic out into the world and give him a chance to see new environments and new possibilities for himself. After all, Skeptics won't just take your word for it.

Sample College List for the Skeptic

Skeptics need to see that there are colleges and universities that are new, unfamiliar, and different than high school. They need to have their preconceived notions about standard paths to college debunked by having different kinds of institutions presented to them; and they'll have to see these places for themselves to believe they're real... The following schools do things differently.

Deep Springs College, CA - if you're up for a mental and physical challenge, Deep Springs, a two-year pre-college, will offer you the opportunity to work on a ranch by day and philosophize in small groups by night. Increasingly tougher to get into, this school recently went co-ed. It attracts students from around the world who are questioning the value of a four-year degree - at least right now. Many of the Deep Springs graduates go on to four-year colleges and universities after completing their very unconventional two-year experience in the desert on the border of California and Nevada. Skeptics will enjoy this unique setting to step back and look at the world with a new set of lenses.

St. John's College, MD - if a return to days of old is what you're seeking, St. John's just may be your best bet. With a curriculum that has changed little since its founding, St. John's seems to be stuck in time with a student body that has an eye on the future. As Donald Asher writes in *Cool Colleges*, St. John's is "an institution that ignores every trend, as if it existed on a separate plane altogether." A *Great Books School*, St. John's students follow the infamous list of *Great Books* throughout their four years there. The classical education offered at St. John's is so old-school that it may very well be the most novel college a Skeptic will come across.

The New School, NYC - Eugene Lang at The New School is the liberal arts college that is often shadowed by the well-known Parsons School of Design, which is also housed at The New School. As a whole, The New School is for free-thinking, independent urbanites who may seek something smaller and a bit quirkier than its neighbor school, NYU. Students here engage in critical inquiry, always contemplating how their studies can be applied in the world and how what their learning can make a real impact. With its urban location and global outlook, The New School attracts students who don't mind the less-than-cohesive and not-so-traditional campus; in fact, I'd say it attracts students who are actively seeking these traits.

Reed College, OR - Scholarship is revered at this simultaneously traditional and progressive institution in Portland. Similar to St. John's in its steadfast curriculum, Reed attracts those quirky and intellectual students who have never fit into any high-school-student categories. There is a nuclear reactor on campus, but it also offers a dance major, and all seniors must submit a final thesis; it's no wonder Reed is one of the top schools for sending graduates into PhD programs. For Skeptics who are craving a community of like-minded scholars who question everything, Reed could be the answer.

Soka University of America - a nod to the Buddhist tradition, Soka University of America promotes global citizenship, awareness, peace, and character development. You don't come to Soka to get ahead; you come to Soka to collaborate and move everyone forward. Soka offers undergraduate degrees with concentrations in Life Sciences, Humanities, International Studies, and Social and Behavioral Sciences, but more than study these subjects, Soka challenges students to gain a better understanding of other cultures and traditions and to contemplate the ways to improve our world. Learning Clusters allow students to work on teams with faculty to tackle tough questions and come up with novel solutions to problems.

4.7 THE INDEPENDENT LEARNER

BEN HAD JUST RETURNED FROM VOLUNTEERING FOR *NO Mas Muertes* (No More Deaths) on the United States-Mexico border in Arizona when we caught up over the phone. *No Mas Muertes* is a volunteer organization that provides relief aid to immigrants coming over the border, and Ben had been with a team providing bottled water. Ben was part of a multi-generational volunteer team, camping along the border, leaving water for immigrants, and replacing water that is dumped out by some Border Patrol Agents.

When I talked to Ben after his trip, he was impassioned. He told me he felt that he had a "moral imperative" to help after learning how bad the situation at the border actually is.

You might sense a little *Hero* in Ben; I sensed the same thing, and remembered how many students feel a need to make a difference (it's one of the magical things about working with teens, who sit at the border of adulthood, but haven't crossed over that border into cynicism). To make a difference, some students navigate through the *establishment* (military) while others, like Ben, prefer the unpaved, winding, and unmapped paths.

Ben felt like he was part of a larger movement, doing something that not only mattered but was life saving. He was also humbled. After long days in the desert, he would sit around campfires with volunteers more knowledgeable and experienced than he, and realize how much he had to learn about immigration, law, diplomacy, and international relations.

Still, Ben wasn't convinced that school was the best place to learn these things. He is articulate, mature, kind, and passionate—not at all the stereotypical rebellious, angry activist who fights all systems and institutions. But he used to be.

Today, Ben is optimistic about future possibilities, deeply connected to a national community of independent learners, activists, musicians, and homesteader-types. Ben is the poster boy for independent learning.

In high school, Ben's parents were more than a little concerned about his apathetic and rebellious streak.

"Do you think you were a rebel in high school?" I asked now-20-year-old Ben over the phone.

"Oh, total rebel," he replied. He remembers joining the football team as a freshman and how his complete resentment toward the sport and his teammates compelled him to run in the opposite direction of the all-American high school teen persona.

"Rebelling in high school is how I was able to cope," he explained.

In an effort to get Ben out of the school environment against which he was increasingly rebelling, his parents enrolled him in a semester-long program called *Unschooling Adventures*, a Colorado-based exploratory program for homeschooled or unschooled high-school students. Blake Boles, founder of the program, now writes and speaks about non-traditional education options, and interviewed Ben for the program.

Ben got nervous in the interview, admitting later that he focused too much on the negative, rather than having an improvement mindset. He was not admitted, but Blake told him, "If you think my decision is bullshit, let me know."

Ben puffed up his chest, renewed his confidence (and optimism), and wrote an email with the subject, "Why I Think Your Decision is Bullshit." Ben was vulnerable and honest in his email; he recounted what he did wrong and why this program was so important to him.

"I was not myself in the interview...I talked more about what I can't do and what I don't like than what I can do and what I do like," he wrote. "I am a novice," he continued, "There is a sense of blind enthusiasm and adoration that someone carries when they are experiencing new opportunities."

He was accepted.

Ben explains the experience as one of belonging. Unlike homeschooling, which often follows a set at-home curriculum, unschooling is a method that allows kids to choose their own direction and learn through living—out there, in the real world.

"Make the most of your freedom" is the tagline on the homepage of *Unschooling Adventures,* a reminder that it's not a given that we're equipped to know exactly what to do when given freedom.

Unschooling can be a difficult transition for students who are used to traditional, structured schooling. There is typically a process of *unlearning* the old ways before a kid can really engage and grow as an unschooler. Unschooling adventures provided Ben with a community.

"Living with these people is what does it for me," he explained. He said that taking his education into his own hands, while exciting, was an "overwhelming prospect."

"It's easier to say 'yes' to a bunch of things when you're around a bunch of people saying 'yes' to those things," he observes.

Peer pressure, most famous for its negative impacts, can turn out to be a net positive when students are encouraged by peers to do things that are good for their development. When Ben returned from his unschooling semester, he was sold on that way of learning: real-world, experiential learning around interesting people with similar values and worldviews. He knew he couldn't go back to traditional schooling after Unschooling Adventures, but he also knew that unschooling on his own would be tough.

His parents enrolled him in an alternative charter high school, yet, even there, Ben recalls, "I was in a comfort zone I didn't want to be in."

What a beautiful way of describing it! While it can be encouraging hanging out in the comfort zone (it's nice for our ego), it doesn't move us forward; it was forward motion that Ben was craving. He dropped out, got his GED, and embarked on a very different path.

It takes great trust in our children—as well as a firm belief that each journey is different—to allow a teenager to do what Ben did. Some of us may have a certain image in our heads of the kid who drops out and gets his GED. Maybe that kid is lazy, unmotivated, or not academically equipped to handle the rigors of high school. Perhaps some people even thought this about Ben at the time. When you talk to him now, you learn very quickly that this young adult has a vocabulary that surpasses not just those of most of his peers' but also most adults'.

Did Ben get this vocabulary from studying flashcards? Definitely not. He's hanging out with people who are smarter and more experienced than he is; he is in the company of people who push him. He knows that, just as skiing with faster skiers will make you a faster skier, traveling, playing music, and volunteering with people who are wiser and more worldly than you, will make you wiser and more worldly, too.

Ben craves new experiences. It's no exaggeration to say he lives for new experiences. He already knows that work, for him, will be a means to fund interesting, challenging, and meaningful life experiences. He doesn't intend to go to college for a *degree*—the degree itself doesn't matter to him. Instead, he wants to attend college for the *experience* he'll have there.

This spring, Ben was accepted to a college that touts experiential learning and a get-your-hands-dirty approach to learning. But he told me that the prospect of going into debt for one life experience, when there are so many other learning experience out there tempting him, doesn't make a lot of sense to him. The whole debt thing is very intimidating for the Independent Learner, who has a hard time imagining himself spending four years immersed in just one experience. For Ben, the most important value guiding his every move is *diversity of experience*, and if college can't offer this, then college isn't for him…at least not right now.

So what happened to the rebellious Ben? He told me that after spending more time outside of school, both with Unschooling Adventures and in the gap year program he did after he got his GED, his rebel mentality started to shift. Once he left the restrictions of formal education, he no longer had something to rebel against. He was hanging out with people who were positive and joyful, following their own paths. Rather than pointing a finger in contempt at the path they'd left, they were looking eagerly toward the future. They knew that everyone must decide for themselves which path is best for them.

Ben shared with me that now he understands that just because traditional school wasn't and isn't right for him, that doesn't mean that path is wrong for everyone. He no longer feels the need to cast shade on the environments, the people, and the methods that didn't serve him, because he now sees that they serve others.

For now, Ben wants to get his driver's license and save some money. He plans to get a car and go back east for a while. He has some friends who can help him retrofit his car to be liveable for a few months. A folk music junkie, he wants to do a work-study with the Campbell Folk Music School in North Carolina. He'd like to play with some of his more talented musician friends in Maine, so he can improve his banjo skills. From there, he thinks he'll go to the Bullock's Permaculture Homestead in Orcas Island, Washington, to do one of their permaculture training programs.

After that, he's determined to get into Deep Springs, the super-competitive, two-year college program listed in the Skeptics chapter (this school is ideal for both student types). He's also applying to a handful of self-directed schools, most of which have organic farms and a decent-sized banjo-playing population.

Guiding the Independent Learner

Not all Independent Learners want to drop out of school, get a GED and learn about banjo-playing and permaculture, but maybe the independent learner you're working with reminds you of Ben in other ways. Some independent learners will struggle in traditional school, leading their parents to think, "My kid will never survive college."

Independent Learners have a lot in common with the Adventurers. Both types can be ideal candidates for homeschooling or unschooling, but don't assume this. Just as Ben and Isabel thought unschooling and homeschooling would be too isolating, community is often very important to these types of students.

Tips and Tactics for Supporting the Independent Learner

- Alternative or flexible schooling options are ideal for these students; to force them to succeed in traditional schooling environments with AP courses and tests will set them up for failure. Remember, these students can be extremely skeptical about higher education or education in general.

- The standard timelines for starting and completing a degree program will be stretched by the Independent Learner, who takes an intuitive, exploratory approach to their education. Patience is key to helping them succeed. Independent Learners only respond well to the deadlines they set for themselves.

- Check out schools with expeditionary learning curricula or those with a combination of in-person and online learning.

- While some Independent Learners are Specialists—experts who go deep into a passion (see chapter 4.4)—many others, like Ben, prefer to "graze." Again, patience is key to supporting their success.

- If you do try homeschooling or unschooling, find co-op groups or meet-ups with similar students in order to create a community for your teen.

Sample College List for the Independent Learner

The Independent Learner wants flexibility, freedom, and the ability to pivot. They want to be able to explore safely, knowing they won't be locked into any path prematurely. Some of these colleges have low-residency options for students who don't want to be on campus full time, while others allow for individualized, customized programs of study. Some of these schools might resemble a kind of institutionalized homeschooling; the opportunity to learn on their own terms, at their own pace, among others who want the same, is exactly what the Independent Learners out there have been wanting.

Goddard College, VT - for those who want to technically "go to college" but who don't really want to be there all of the time, Goddard was made for you. A "low-residency" school, Goddard has a mix of on-campus and off-campus learning opportunities for students. Though not a place for those seeking a true college community, this school is perfect for those students who are used to—and prefer—working independently, and for those who don't want college to interfere with life.

The Evergreen State College, WA - This small, public, unconventional school in Olympia, Washington replaced "Courses" with "Programs," which students enroll in for the entire term and are interdisciplinary, and team taught. For example, "Visualizing Microbial Seascapes: An Introduction to Animation and Marine Biology," and "Business: Innovation, Stewardship, and Change" were recent programs that students could take. Known for its liberal—and environmental ideals—it's no wonder that Evergreen has its own organic plant and animal farm.

University of Washington - You might not expect an Independent Learner to choose one of the largest, most conventional schools in the country, but hear me out. UW has a unique academic program called the Individualized Learning Plan for which students must go through a rigorous application process. As part of the application, prospective students design their own interdisciplinary course of study in the liberal arts. The program reminds students that this program is not for those seeking professional *training*, rather, it's for those seeking a unique, broad, and individualized *education*.

Marlboro College - Similar to other schools with working farms, Marlboro lives by a "get your hands dirty" mantra. Additionally, all students at Marlboro pursue a self-designed "Plan of Concentration" based on their own interests and passions. At the end of their studies, students do a final scholarly project to demonstrate their mastery. Plans of Concentration are usually interdisciplinary, so you might have a student dipping into mathematics, science, dance, and theater. A beautiful spider-web design on the Marlboro website provides an excellent demonstration of the incredible variety of subject combinations students have created over the years.

New College of Florida - Considered the honors college in the Florida state higher education system, New College of Florida will feel like a small, private liberal arts college. It will also feel a bit more like graduate school with its emphasis on independent research and student-driven learning. The school has gotten rid of traditional grading and GPAs, opting instead for comprehensive narrative evaluation. Their logic? Focus on the work and the learning, not the grades, and give students the freedom to craft their own educational experience.

CHAPTER 5

The Best-Laid Plans

I t would be a huge failure on my part if, after reading these case studies, recommendations, and opinions, you thought that putting them into practice in your—or your student's—life would invariably lead to happiness and success. Even if the plan you put into place seems like the authentic "best fit" plan, things can go, well, not as planned.

Recently, I was speaking at college-prep high school in Chicago and after my talk, a parent asked, "So, let's say our kids do all of this stuff; they take all of the 'right' classes and do the community service, but then are ultimately rejected from their first-choice schools. Is it just like, oh well!? Too Bad?" At first, I didn't think I heard the question correctly. She directed her concern at the high school's counselor, so I decided to let her take that one. But here's what I wanted to say:

As soon as you get home, I want you to run to your kid and hug him and tell him you love him. Then, tell him that he can have the loftiest goals and plans that he can dream up—fancy colleges, high-paying jobs, flights around the world—and you will of course support him and cheer him on. But then tell him to not ever, EVER, think that the work he puts into his goals was wasted just because the goals don't come to fruition.

I have had students voice similar concerns. "If I don't get into an Ivy, all of my hard work in high school will have been a waste." Yikes. This is dangerous thinking. Let's curtail this.

The story I am about to share with you is not as uplifting as the others I've shared so far. There isn't a happy ending (yet) to this story. But in a way, this story is the happiest, most uplifting of them all. And it comes from a very wise, very humble, and very happy 19-year-old.

"We *were* kind of like sheep in high school," Abby told me when I asked her about her high-school years. I interviewed her in the noisy coffee shop near her home about 45 minutes east of South Lake Tahoe. I sipped coffee and recorded the interview on my phone while she sat smiling across from me with nothing to drink or eat. "Do you want something," I asked. "Oh right, I forgot. Sorry." Abby couldn't have anything.

"We were all in it together," she continued. "We were all like minded. It was easy to conform to what everyone else was doing. The AP test was the big thing at the end of the year that we all worked toward. You didn't want to fall short of what anyone else was doing." Abby now reflects on how bizarre the whole sheep-herding business was back in high school. But Abby was happily part of it back then, so on she charged. She kept up with the herd that collectively patted itself on the back when teachers remarked, "This is the best class we've seen in years!"

In his book, *Excellent Sheep: The Miseducation of the American Elite and the Way to a Meaningful Life*, William Deresiewicz explains that the human habit of blindly following the herd is particularly harmful when it comes to teens and the college admission craze. The Cult of College Prestige has young people tripping over themselves for reasons they can't articulate (or for reasons that, if voiced out loud, would sound every bit as nuts as they really are). Deresiewicz reminds us that the good and studious kids are indeed, quite excellent, but that doesn't make them any less *sheeplike*. They're the most intelligent and best-performing sheep. But they are still, well, sheep.

Abby had high expectations for herself. Her future always seemed not only bright, but utterly predictable and within her control.

"I loved sports, I loved school, I was very studious," she says. This drive motivated her to do well in school. She got As and Bs, took a heavy load of honors and AP classes, and did all the right extracurriculars: sports, clubs, and community service (she even trained a guide dog for the blind). "I always had a drive to do good in the world and to do good for myself."

Earlier in life, when Abby was nine years old, she had a wrist injury that never fully healed. This was weird, but not totally debilitating. She regained the strength in her wrist, later building a makeshift climbing wall in her attic to hone her skills at home after climbing practice at the gym.

But there were other strange things she began to notice, which worsened as she entered high school. Her symptoms were hard to explain and the doctors couldn't make sense of her vague descriptions of abnormal symptoms. And when you can't really explain what your body is going through, and doctors can't give you a definitive word for what you are going through, you make do, albeit with some annoyance and frustration.

"I was diagnosed ten times over, and the doctors all kind of had conflicting views," she told me. In fact, Abby has multiple complex chronic illnesses and genetic conditions, all of which seem to interrelate, triggering each other like a messy anatomical pinball machine. She still doesn't have a crystal clear understanding of what her body is trying to tell her through all of the debilitating symptoms, but she is learning more about anatomy and physiology than most people her age, she optimistically points out.

The virtual house-arrest that comes with her required level of care has certainly curtailed the freedom she imagined having at this time in her life. Rock climbing would have to wait. This uncertainty about the future came as a hard blow to a girl who had always succeeded because she knew the steps, followed the rules, did her work, and paid attention to the details.

Leading up to graduation, Abby didn't want to admit to herself that her illness was going to get in the way of her longest-term dream: going to college. Abby could see her end goal; she had been admitted to a selective college in the midwest. But as summer approached it became clear that this thing she had devoted so much time and energy to was not going to be the reward at the end of the finish line.

Suddenly, her priorities had to shift.

"Everyday was—well it still is—one minute after the next," she told me.

Abby abruptly transitioned from planning for her future to planning for the day.

These days, Abby wakes up at 4 o'clock each morning to begin her daily routine: prayer, meditation, taking supplements and medications, getting her medical devices and equipment ready, and getting herself up and ready. This takes four to five hours. The rest of the day is spent completing coursework for her online class at the local community college, reading, and playing with her new puppy...all while living at home...with her parents. Not at all the life the 19-year-old planned to live after her high-school graduation.

Today, when Abby hears the woes of her college friends, complaining about roommates or homework, she envies them. "Those," she laughs, "are normal issues. I want *those* issues."

The best-laid plans of mice and men often go awry.

Abby came to understand this quote sooner than most. It took time, but Abby now says, "It came down to faith and self belief, I think. I had to let go of what everyone else expected of me."

In one of Abby's college application essays she wrote, "Essentially, there's an ideal perception of what a successful life is supposed to be and a staircase of milestones that must be met along the way."

Through Abby's illness, she had to change her perspective about the way things are "supposed to go." She now sees clearly the pressure that society placed on her to live a certain way. She understands, better than most, that when it doesn't go this way, it's easy to feel like we've failed. She believes that, when you take a step back, "any way is the right way to go for you."

"I always had a strong faith…but it was more like church on Sundays. Faith plays a role in everyday life for me now," she says. The well-known phrase, "God never gives you more than you can handle" has taken on a new meaning for Abby. There were days when she really did not feel like she could handle what she had to face.

"People look at you like you're strong when you feel your weakest," she tells me. She came to realize that the ordeal she was going through was not necessarily meant to make her a tough fighter or a slayer of weakness; quite the opposite. The thing she was going through taught her to surrender, and for her that meant relinquishing her struggle to a higher power. She realized that to assume she could handle this nightmare on her own was to assume she was in control—and she most certainly was not.

But Abby discovered "beauty in being torn apart," as she puts it. In trusting the journey (whether or not one believes that journey laid out by a higher power, or somehow predetermined), she found a sense of relief and calm. More importantly, Abby was, through her illness, forced to stop controlling, planning, and predicting. She was challenged to start living her life instead.

And very importantly, Abby experienced something we all crave: release from comparison. She couldn't physically keep up with her peers anymore; it was simply impossible for her to live the lives they were living. She had no other choice but to focus on her own life.

Abby's journey profoundly affected me, and helped bring into focus a thought that had been incubating in me throughout my work with future-focused, obsessively planning high school kids. They didn't come up with this system, after all. If they felt they really had a choice, would they sign up for the grueling grind that is the Cult of College Prestige? Probably not.

Abby's story is a dramatic one, but it offers a lesson for all of us. We shouldn't have to endure a massive health crisis to realize that we can't engineer perfect life outcomes. Releasing the illusion of control and the tyranny of comparison to others will enable us all—parents and students alike—to live our lives more fully, and with greater appreciation for our unique paths.

Surprisingly, hitting a lower rock bottom than she ever thought possible helped Abby forge remarkable self confidence. She learned how to advocate for herself as she bounced from one doctor to the next. She learned how to speak up for herself because her life, not just a grade, was on the line.

In high school, Abby had been convinced she'd go to medical school. This path sounded reasonable and responsible. Today, however, her life looks so different, and so too do her plans. She has a new perspective on doing the things she loves, rather than the things that simply sound "responsible." She has come to see that it's okay to "figure it out as you go" and not commit to a specific, narrow path right away.

What's Abby's advice to high-school students stuck in the college admission hamster wheel, living to please those around them and killing themselves to keep up with their peers?

"Find the people who stand with you during your worst moments...stand with you *and* make you laugh!" she says, smiling. Most of all, she sees the importance of doing what we love *now*—because none of us know how long we have.

"Tomorrows aren't guaranteed," she reminds me. "Doing what you love is what matters. No matter what you're interested in, it's going to work out. Financially it's going to work out, and spiritually it's going to work out."

CHAPTER 6

The Pursuit of Happiness

W hy *don't* we consistently and mindfully pursue the things that make us happy, and encourage our kids to do the same? Perhaps it's because we consider ourselves "realists" or "pragmatists," and believe we're looking after their best interests. Indeed, I'm sure Abby's words will strike many of you as naive, or just a response to her extreme life circumstances.

At the end of the day, we tell ourselves, life is complicated. The world is competitive. We want our kids to deal with the real-world business of getting a good job and making a living *first*, and save that pursuit-of-happiness stuff for their spare time.

But let's consider, for a moment, our cultural misapprehensions about happiness. Perhaps it's a poor understanding of happiness that makes us judge people as naive when they appear to over value that emotional state. We may tend to think of a person focused on happiness as a sort of frivolous Pollyanna, skipping around, oblivious to what's "really" going on. But happiness is something much more pragmatic than this, and a new understanding of it could help us really *mean* it when we say, "I just want my kid to be happy."

The World Happiness index was inspired by a United Nations resolution to start considering and measuring "Gross Domestic Happiness" as a holistic way of determining priorities in social and economic policy. The Happiness Index is conducted annually and measures an array of factors, including GDP per capita, healthy life expectancy, social support, and freedom to make life choices. It also asks citizen-respondents to consider the "best possible lives" for themselves and rate their actual lives on a scale of 0 (worst possible life) to 10 (best possible life).

Would it surprise you to learn that life-liberty-and-the-pursuit-of-happiness United States ranks 18th in the World Happiness Index? Finland, Norway and Denmark hold the top 3 spots. While the subjectivity of the Index's criteria remains somewhat controversial, in large part due to its focus on material measures over emotional ones, it's an interesting glimpse into national priorities.

A couple of years ago I was working with two brothers who were not too excited to be working with me. Planning for college was the last thing they wanted to do. I respected where they were, and as I tried to understand more about their interests, hobbies, and side projects, I learned that the older brother really enjoyed working on cars. Pretty normal for a teenage boy—yet how many parents would say, "Jimmy, what can we do to help you dive even deeper into this hobby of yours? How can we help you become the best auto mechanic around? How could you make this craft your own?"

Certainly not their mother. She was, in a word, intense. Rarely did a smile appear on her face.

"I really just want my boys to be happy," she said sternly, her words belying the tone of her voice.

It seemed to me that she really *did* just want her boys to be happy, but fear about the future and the unknown had her doubling down on them, getting on them about homework, grades, and courses (not to mention signing them up for college counseling at the very beginning of high school).

Then she added, in the next breath, "But I've told them that if they really want job security, they should become nurses."

The bubble burst.

Since then, I've worked with many parents who, consciously or not, attempt to dictate their kids' educational and career paths. To them, it's a natural extension of their parenting responsibilities, even as their kids are preparing to leave the nest. These well-meaning folks really do believe *their* plans will lead to a better life for their kids than their kids' own plans (or lack thereof). Mother knows best, right?

As a parent, I believe that most of us truly do want our kids to be happy and fulfilled. It's just that we often disagree with our kids about the root of happiness or how to "achieve" happiness.

Take the statement, "We've told John he can't be an art major because we don't want him living in our basement after graduation." A pretty popular sentiment—you've probably heard things like this, or even said things like this! But ultimately, it stems from a deep love for John. Job one in every parent's book is ensuring that our kids are safe and secure.

John's parents, and most other parents, want their kids to achieve independence, financial security, and self sufficiency. From their vantage point, this is what's necessary in order to be happy. In my work, it's tempting to dismiss some parents' hopes for their kids as a form of wish fulfillment: they want their offspring to be wealthy and powerful. But I've come to understand that the root of that desire is for their offspring to be happy. They simply *think* wealth and power will do the trick.

Most of us want our kids to be better off than we are, but it's easy to get derailed as we think about what will make our kids "better off." Is it more money? A more fulfilling job? More time with their family and friends? More opportunities to travel? A more rewarding education? More time to volunteer?

What we parents need to reflect on (ideally *before* we start talking to our teens about college and career pathways) is how we might be living vicariously through our children. How might we be trying to fill happiness gaps in our own lives by directing our children down particular paths? Our kids, we think, are part of us, and it's difficult to separate our own hopes, fears, biases, and desires from theirs.

Many parents who are knee deep in the high-stakes, high-stress job of parenting teens feel like taking their hands off the wheel for a moment could result in a mistake with life-long implications. But our job as parents is not to completely shield our children from everything that does not resemble utter and complete happiness. Many rewarding destinations require some pretty treacherous paths. We can, instead, give our kids tools to help them on their journey. We can give them the wherewithal to pick a direction, walk towards it, change direction, and keep pushing on. We can encourage them even if they change direction several more times, walk several more miles, and then realize the first path, (maybe one from 25 years ago!) was actually the best one.

Jennifer Michael Hecht, author of *The Happiness Myth*, believes that, "the basic modern assumptions about how to be happy are nonsense." In a review of her book for *The New York Times*, Alison McCulloch summed it up, "What you think you should do to be happy, like getting fitter and thinner, is part of a 'cultural code' — 'an unscientific web of symbolic cultural fantasies' — and once you realize this, you will perhaps feel a little more free to be a lot more happy."[21]

In his book *The Happiness Trap*, Dr. Russ Harris talks about the "Happiness Myth." The myth is that, just as every love story and Disney movie ends with "happily ever after," so too must our lives. Just as problematic, everything has to be super happy all the time—and if it's not, something's wrong. The Happiness Myth insists that we should be able to control our thoughts and feelings, to make them happy thoughts and feelings. This is the trap. Our minds, Dr. Harris explains, are evolutionarily designed as "don't-get-killed" devices. Worry, concern, and other "negative" emotions can serve a practical, protective function. Failing to achieve something often sets us on a different and ultimately better path. Instead of attempting to force our minds into a constant state of happiness, we need to accept that some negativity is a natural part of life. His recommendation: commit to living a *values-driven* life—instead of a purely goals-driven life.

Could you imagine how different high-school and college experiences would be if instead of working towards goals "out there," like the *ideal* college, job, house, car, or future spouse, students lived in accordance with their own established values and worked towards creating a life that included their core values? How different would the college-admissions process look if this was the case?

Instead of asking, "Where do you want to go?" or "Who do you want to be?" or "What do you want to do?" we should be asking students, "What matters to you?" and "How do you want to show up in the world?" This way, when your child feels like they've just had major failure, you can ask them if their

---

21 McCulloch, Alison (May 6, 2007). "Get Happy". The New York Times Sunday Book Review. The New York Times Company. Retrieved 9 March 2014

actions aligned with their values. If the answer is "yes," then perhaps what they've just experienced was uncomfortable, but not truly a failure. If however, the answer is "no," then there's an opportunity to realign with internal values, not an opportunity to chase an external goal with newfound aggression (which is the way many of us view failures).

Last year, I was asked by my friend and colleague, Molly Dahl, to accompany her on a trip to Germany for a Positive Psychology conference. Molly is an expert practitioner in the field of Positive Psychology and author of YOUTH Positive, a social and emotional learning curriculum for schools. I am not an expert in this space, however, I majored in German and she wanted me to help with translations (see, those liberal arts degrees really do come in handy!) According to the Positive Psychology Institute, "Positive Psychology is the scientific study of human flourishing, and an applied approach to optimal functioning. It has also been defined as the study of the strengths and virtues that enable individuals, communities and organizations to thrive."[22]

I was glad to tag along, especially because Molly is one of the loveliest humans I know, which you'd probably expect from someone who has studied Positive Psychology. While listening to truly fascinating, engaging speakers, I was translating as quickly as I could for Molly, who looked over my shoulder to read what I was typing, as I explained why people were laughing, arguing, crying, or gasping about something a speaker said. I sat down with Molly after the conference to figure out what we could learn from Positive Psychology in the context of college admissions.

---

22 www.positivepsychologyinstitute.com

"Positive Psychology—and our grandmother—reminds us that the world is our oyster: that it's a good place, filled with good people, all of us trying to do our best to be happy, to find fulfillment, and to make a contribution. The old adage 'bloom where you're planted' comes to mind. Happiness does not exist *out there*," she maintained.

Molly explained to me that research has shown that happy people are more successful—financially, in their relationships, in their careers—not that successful people are happy.

"The saying 'money can't buy happiness' has been scientifically proven," she laughed. "So, what if we re-imagine how we define success?"

Today's college-bound kids, she explained, are under tremendous pressure to get into the best school, so they can get the best job, and achieve the best life—an equation that they believe will bring happiness. Unfortunately, it doesn't work that way. Happiness is a journey, not a destination. Happiness does not lie beyond some mythical goal line, which the Prestige College grad will triumphantly sprint across.

The Cult of College Prestige continues, she explains, because "we love 'badges.' Being a part of a prestigious university is a badge of external acceptance. But, research, dating back to the 1970s, stresses the importance of learning self acceptance. As we grow up, we need approval and acceptance from others; our parents, first and foremost; our peers and classmates; our teachers. But as we move beyond the elementary-school classroom, we need to develop the "soft" skill of self acceptance."

A retired teacher, Molly observes that today's youth haven't been presented with authentic opportunities to develop this crucial skill.

"Authentic self acceptance is an individual knowing that he or she is okay, that there is nothing fundamentally wrong with them, that he or she is enough, and that they have a unique contribution to make in the world."

She continues, "It may sound surprising, but that comes from failing and getting back up and trying again—as many times as it takes to find success. It comes from hard work and determination. It requires resilience and perspective-taking. It comes from having to do things by ourselves. It comes from learning to fail, so we do not fail to learn."

As you may have guessed, Positive Psychology is not the often-derided "Self Esteem" movement (a kissing cousin of the Happiness Myth). There's nothing wrong with promoting kids' self esteem—but without the ability to withstand and learn from failure, it's a thin veneer that's easily cracked. Confidence is cultivated, not by receiving constant positive reinforcement, but by grappling with and overcoming challenges.

Positive Psychology can also be misunderstood as a sort of Pollyanna perspective, the art of *acting* happy when things are crummy. But Positive Psychology acknowledges and embraces the inevitable struggle and the messiness of life and provides ways to find authentic joy in the midst of that.

The lessons of Positive Psychology can be a boon for teens wondering how to build a bridge to a life after high school. It can help frame conversations around success, achievement, and what we define as "making it." This time in a teen's life might be the most urgent time to have these conversations—ideally *before* a flood of possible rejection letters from admissions offices hit the mailbox.

Wouldn't it be great if we could have these conversations with young people sooner? We have the opportunity to help students avoid forming limited views of success—the belief that a certain few colleges will make them happy, make them wealthy, or give them more respect from their peers.

I confess, my work entails bursting many a bubble. After years of AP courses, comparing themselves to their classmates, studying endlessly for countless standardized tests, students may hear for the first time—from Yours Truly—that all this competition, effort, and anxiety doesn't actually lead to a magical moment when they're granted happiness, success, and satisfaction.

When I share this information with a student (I do try to be gentle!) I get a range of responses: frustration, blank stares, the occasional expletive, and even screaming into pillows. I've had students tell me that if they couldn't get into one of the most selective schools in the country, then all of their laboring, late nights, and obedience would be for *nothing*. It's stunning to see these promising young people, just starting their lives, believing that those very lives are essentially over if they can't join the Cult of College Prestige. What a depressing thought!

If a student (or her family) is dead set on getting into one of those schools that prides itself on the number of students it *rejects* rather than accepts, then I advise them to tread cautiously—to frame the process as an exciting challenge, but nothing more.

It's extremely risky to place our hopes for happiness, success, and satisfaction in the hands of these institutions. So first, we need to understand how we can feel these things regardless of what's going on *out there*. Instead of looking outward, attempting to latch on to an imagined, external source of happiness, we need to understand what makes us happy, what energizes us, what ignites our passions.

Naturally, most adults are still trying to figure this all out ourselves, so why would we expect teenagers to receive some sort of magical download of knowledge about what to do and where to go?

CHAPTER 7

Step Away from Fear-Based Planning

R emember Amanda from the Introduction? She started out as a gregarious, probing, questioning teen, but changed during the writing of this book.

Amanda found that the stresses of beginning her senior year at a pressure-cooker high school, combined with the loaded, emotionally fraught college visit with her mom, only worked to elevate her anxieties. Amanda shut down. The fiercely independent student I knew in the first few sessions became unresponsive and stopped the college-planning journey altogether.

In retrospect, I wonder if there wasn't more I could have done to calm her overwhelm, but I learned the seeds were planted long ago: a mom who, with the best intentions, insisted on her learning to read by kindergarten and obsessed over her daughter's "deficiencies," rattling off a list of diagnoses and learning disorders at our first meeting, as if these were her daughter's only defining attributes.

Rather than seek out a more conducive learning environment than the intensely competitive high school she attended, Amanda's parents encouraged her to stick with it and uphold the long family legacy at the school. It's no wonder that the perfect storm of stress variables at the beginning of senior year caused Amanda to crawl into a cave.

Make the shift from seeing the college admission journey as a defining life event that occurs on a one-size-fits-all path to viewing it as a thing you *do*—an activity, an adventure. Parents who restrict their students' options after high school are at risk of disempowering them to the point of inducing debilitating anxiety and depression. How do we know this? Students admitted to high-intensity, pressure-cooker colleges are leaving early. They're returning to the comforts of home, realizing that they were not prepared for, or suited to, such a stressful college environment.

Students whose parents and teachers never fostered individual agency—opting instead for a form of parenting and educating that dictates to the child what to do, when to do it, and how to do it—are finding out much too late that the young person cannot make even simple decisions on their own.

Fear is causing parents to relive their youth, and to avoid mistakes they made themselves, by living vicariously through their children. Fear is causing parents to say things like, "*We* won't be applying there. *I've* never heard of it," as if both the student and parent will be rooming together in a double dorm room in college. Fear is causing parents to submit college applications on their student's behalf (while not sharing the passwords to the applicant portals with their student). Fear is causing parents to write their child's college admission essays, proudly using words like "cacophonous," "blithely," and "thusly." They don't realize that these little red flags not only elicit eye rolls from college admissions officers, but also reveal the sad reality that these parents do not trust their child to tell his own story in his own words. Fear is taking the journey, the adventure, and the excitement out of the whole process, tricking all of us into believing that it can be more predictable, more controlled, and more black-and-white; in other words, less human.

But the truth is, young and vulnerable humans put their all into college applications that are reviewed by other humans; humans then make decisions about other humans—it's a messy and imperfect process. However, it does not have to be devastating and fear inducing; our young people don't need to put their self worth and life goals in the hands of a few application readers who will never meet them. Instead, students can choose to consider a wider array of options—options that are better, more natural fits—that will not require them to change who they are.

When we think clearly, we all know that the options available to high-school graduates today are *limitless*; this endlessness is actually causing another kind of anxiety and overwhelm (but that's a topic for another book). What should not be causing sleeplessness is the false notion that the options are *limited*, finite, structured, and clear. Each path to college (even the well-trodden one) is an experiment, just as every life is.

One thing I *have* found to be remarkably consistent in the college-planning journey is this: the students whose parents take a back seat in the process, only helping when asked by the student, have the best experience by far. There is more clarity, less stress; essays are more honest, and believe it or not, materials are submitted in a more timely manner. In a very practical sense, relaxed parents allow their kids to be more "on top of it." But more importantly, relaxed parents send a quiet but profound message to their kids: "I trust you."

CHAPTER 8

Go Your Own Way

O ne of the great privileges of my work is getting to know so many remarkable young people. And my final story illustrates one of the most important ideas I've shared in this book: that all students are unique and must discover their own unique paths to adulthood. Libby, a Nordic (cross-country) skier, was no exception.

In my work, I've met two types of student athletes: those who say they will do college sports "if the opportunity arises," but who don't want athletics to be the main part of their college experience, and those who say they're *only* going to college to be an athlete; it's all or nothing. The former usually end up doing Division 3 (D3), club, or intramural sports, while the latter shoot for Division 1 (D1) athletics. In my experience, when a student says she only wants to go to college if she can do her sport, she ends up getting recruited by a D1 school.

Libby was that second type of Athlete, but her intense competitive spirit was blended with kindness. Always smiling, she wore her blond hair in a low ponytail (not the high ponytail of her soccer-playing friends.) When Libby decided to focus her attention on skiing rather than soccer, she adopted the low pony—a habit she continued even when she wasn't wearing her ski beanie.

Libby grew up in the Sierra Nevada mountains, north of Lake Tahoe, where kids learn to ski as soon as they can walk. Competitive skiing is huge in this part of the country, and for those kids who have not been skiing since they were in diapers, fitting in can be tough. Young competitive skiers, can attend special ski academies, unconventional high schools that have flexible curricula and schedules to accommodate students who compete on an international level. Still, it's rare to see a student fight hard to get recruited to a D1 Nordic ski team (there are not many such teams to begin with and the sport doesn't carry the same popularity as, say, football).

For Libby, the long, tiresome process of getting the attention of coaches while also completing her applications for college reminded her a lot of bad high-school dating. "I want you to want me!" she recalls thinking, when I talked to her about this over the phone. The back-and-forth emails and calls required of serious prospective recruits vying for a coveted spot on the team, were exhausting. Libby would come to me wondering if she was pestering them too much.

"I just talked to the coach on Wednesday and he said he would get back to me by the end of the day. It's Friday and I haven't heard from him. Is it weird if I email him again?" she'd fret. "I don't want to be annoying!"

I would always reassure Libby that she wasn't being annoying. Ultimately, this squeaky wheel did get the grease. Libby got into her first-choice school and team—University of Vermont—but not in the conventional way. She was accepted to UVM around March, but that admission did not come with a spot on the ski team. The coach told her the only way she would get a spot that year was if another skier backed out, which he said was not likely.

Libby was deflated, but she'd already made up her mind that UVM was where she needed to be. She began talking to a program director about the possibility of taking a "PG Year." It is not uncommon for athletes to take a postgraduate year off before college in order to improve in their sport and try again for a spot on a team the next year. Libby was beginning to get excited about this option to ski full time after high school and improve enough to be a more qualified athlete at UVM the following year. But she didn't have to wait that long.

On a road trip with her family to the California coast during spring break of her senior year, her phone rang—it was the UVM ski coach. Libby signaled for her mother to pull over. She answered, going quiet for a moment, and then screamed with excitement and relief. She'd gotten a spot on the UVM Nordic ski team after all.

Her relief and joy were audible when we spoke shortly after the call, but Libby's humility meant that instead of pride, she overflowed with gratitude. Today, she still expresses that gratitude, having no complaints about her college experience, since she feels so lucky to have secured a spot on the team. Because Libby had reconciled herself to a long delay, the surprise acceptance was that much more thrilling.

Libby's unique blend of flexibility, which stemmed from her gracious nature, and tenacity, which was the root of her athletic excellence, enabled her to fulfill her dream.

Student athletes provide a particularly interesting cross section of the entire student landscape, because they weave together such a broad combination of archetypes. Athletes can be driven like Achievers, focused like Specialists, and often display the loyalty and personal discipline of Heroes. Many of them crave new experiences like Adventurers, and love traveling to compete in tournaments and races around the world.

I've worked with athletes who were musicians and writers, debaters and doubters, straight-A students at college-prep high schools and homeschooled students. Many of us were athletes at one point in our lives, though few of us made the intense commitment required of recruited college athletes.

Libby is also a wonderful reminder that there are students who want to go to college for reasons other than academics, Greek life, or location. Students like Libby show us that our deepest goals are worth fighting for, even when the path to them is unclear, or appears to be closed off completely.

"Going your own way" often means navigating unexpected obstacles, as it did for Libby. To be true to her chosen path, she was willing to wait. The typical, fiercely binary college-application process (accepted/rejected, win/lose) sets many students up for disappointment and frustration. For kids to chart their own course, resilience, resourcefulness, and flexibility are characteristics that must be cultivated and celebrated. And as much as parents would like to get that College Thing off their list of concerns, getting it right is more important that getting it done.

I hope this book has provided a glimpse into the myriad paths to consider after high school. Hopefully, reading about students' stories and experiences gives you a sense of comfort and the sense that any desired and mindful path *really can work*.

This book is intended to *open the door* to the possibilities; these students and their stories aren't intended to serve as templates to be reproduced. I've shared their experiences to show you what's possible and what's worked for other students, often despite the doubts and judgements of friends, family, and teachers. These stories are meant to encourage you and help you think more broadly about the options, rather than give you an exact blueprint to follow.

This type of student-centered college guidance, while ideal, is not realistic for most counselors at American high schools today. With the average counselor-to-student ratio at public high schools nearly 1 to 500, it's easy to understand why we look for clear roadmaps to college, and embrace simple answers to big, messy questions about the future. It's time consuming to personalize this process. For most school counselors, even the very best ones, it's just not realistic to really get to know every student and then curate opportunities that are a perfect fit for each.

Few among us can describe our personalities, needs, and desires in simple words; indeed, many of us struggle to find the words altogether. We can't quite articulate why we're not drawn to service or why we are, why we hate creating visual projects or why we love them. Discovering the language to talk about ourselves is like knowing enough French to get to the bathroom, board a train, and order a croissant in France—it's downright liberating!

This is how other adults in students' lives can help. Every parent, mentor, older sibling, and teacher can play a vital role. I invite every caring adult to take one student (or more!) under his or her wing, really get to know those students, and listen to their hopes and dreams. And then, hopefully with the new perspectives provided here, you can help guide them across the bridge between high school and college—or more accurately, the bridge between high school and adult life. This doesn't require that you be an expert on college admission yourself, but that you serve as a Guide, undertaking the journey with them and providing them the space and encouragement needed to fully explore their options.

My deepest hope is that students will stop wondering *how to get into college* and instead, with the help of their Guides, begin crafting a deeply personalized path that allows them to go their own way, and to thrive.

ACKNOWLEDGEMENTS

~~~~~~

When I first set out to put all of my random opinions, observations, and student stories into a book, I got to about 70 pages and thought, this is all I got. It wasn't all I had in me, but I needed a community of people to remind me of my voice, my passion, and my enthusiasm for this project. Peggy Wynn Borgman, my content editor and creative coach, was an invaluable member of that community. Without her humor, honesty, encouragement, and quick and accurate eye, this book would not exist. My book cover designer and long-time design team, Laxalt and McIver, designed a cover draft for me early on as a way to make this thing a bit more real for me. Seeing it made me believe in it more. They beautifully captured my messy and abstract vision in my head.

Over the years, I have relied on college visits and student testimonials to inform my research. I've also relied on resources like *College Planner Pro*, *The Fiske Guide*, *The College Board*, and *YouScience* in my daily work and for this book.

Adam Robinson, my book developer, instantly understood my style and approach, and he took on this project with enthusiasm and speed. I am so grateful to him, and others like him, who support and encourage the solopreneurs out there who can often feel like tiny islands in a vast ocean.

While my husband, Jonas Ellison, is a copywriter, he was not *my* copywriter (after ten years of marriage, I wasn't about to end it all over word choice disagreements), but he lovingly did the final read-through of my manuscript, offering the gentlest of criticisms. But most importantly, he kept me moving through those frequent valleys of doubt. He reminded me that, even though working on this book felt like a luxury I couldn't indulge in, it was important and worth it. Thank you. I love you.

Finally, and most obviously, I am indebted to the students and parents who agreed to be interviewed for this book. I am grateful for the opportunity to have been a part of your journey, and equally grateful that you let me share your journeys with others. I know your stories will inspire, motivate and reassure others, and remind the readers that they are not alone in their fears and celebrations. Without your graciousness and openness to retell your paths, this project would have remained an idea. Thank you.

Made in the USA
Middletown, DE
11 July 2019